Features a simulated interview with God
based on His Holy Words as recorded
in the NIV of the Bible

Author shares experiences and ideas about Christian faith

Some portions are written in conversational style

Jim Edwards

THE FINAL WORD

iUniverse books may be ordered through booksellers or by contacting:

iUniverse
1663 Liberty Drive
Bloomington, IN 47403
www.iuniverse.com
1-800-Authors (1-800-288-4677)

ISBN: 978-1-5320-1096-5 (sc)
ISBN: 978-1-5320-1095-8 (e)

Library of Congress Control Number: 2016920765

Print information available on the last page.

iUniverse rev. date: 12/19/2016

To whomever you are from the author:
"May the force of God be with you!"
Jim Edwards

NOTICE

Quoted scriptures in this book are taken from the NEW INTERNATIONAL VERSION (NIV) of the Holy Bible provided by the generosity of the World Bible School. Less than 500 verses that account for less than 25 percent of the total text of work in this book are used directly (verbatim) from the NIV of the Holy Bible.

Disclosures

Scripture taken from THE HOLY BIBLE, NEW INTERNATIONAL VERSION*.

*"NIV" and "NEW INTERNATIONAL VERSION" are trademarks registered in the United States Patent and Trademark office by International Bible Society.

Non-quoted words reflecting what God inspired the writers of the Bible to say are paraphrased based on a consultative synthesis covering portions of approximately 25 versions of translations of the Holy Bible, in addition to the New International Version (NIV), including:

- the American Standard (ASV),
- Revised Standard (RSV),
- (Revised Good News (RGN),

- Living Bible (LB),
- King James (KJ),
- New king James (NKJV),
- New American Standard Bible: New Testament (NASB),
- Amplified New Testament (Amp),
- New English Bible: New Testament (NEB),
- New Testament of Our Lord and Savior Jesus Christ by John Broadus et al (ABUV),
- New Testament by Henry Alford (Alf),
- New Testament in Basic English (Bas),
- New Testament in the Language of Today by William F. Beck (Beck),
- Berkeley Version of the New Testament by Gerrit Verkuyl (Ber),
- Epistles of Paul by W.J. Conybeare (Con),
- New Testament: An American Translation by Edgar J. Goodspeed (Gspd),
- New Testament in the Translation of Monsignor Ronald Knox (Knox),
- New Testament According to the Eastern Texts by George N. Lamas (Lam),
- New Testament: A New Translation by James Moffatt (Mof),
- Centenary Translation: The New Testament in Modern English by Helen Bartlett Montgomery (Mon),
- New Testament: A New Translation by Olaf M. Norlie (Nor),
- New Testament in Modern English by J.B. Phillips (Phi),
- Book of Acts by C.H. Rieu (Rieu),
- Emphasized New Testament: A New Translation by H,B. Rotherham (Rhm),

- Living Letters: The Paraphrased Epistles; Living Gospels; The Paraphrased Gospels; Living Prophecies; The Minor Prophets Paraphrased and Daniel and the Revelation by Kenneth N. Taylor (Tay),
- Twentieth Century New Testament (TCNT),
- New Testament in Modern Speech by Richard Francis Weymouth (Wey), and
- New Testament: A Translation in the Language of the People by Charles B. Williams (Wms).

Most of the images in this book were provided by Tony Bosley at RetroClipArt.com. The remaining images are either in the public domain or were prepared by the author.

THIS BOOK IS DEDICATED TO MY FAMILY.

After God, Jesus and the Holy Spirit my love can be no greater for my wife, Virginia Ann (Mama Toots); sons, Bo and Chad Edwards; daughters, Calli Ann Wilson and Judy Clair Turbeville; grandchildren, Reagin Edwards, Lee Wilson, Caroline Turbeville, and Reese Edwards; my son-in-law, William Wilson; and my first-cousins, Lamar McEachern and Marion McEachern. *"I love you with all that I am!"*

My desire to write this book is inspired by my grandson Lee. He is a special person who knows God in ways that are different than many of us. Lee provides me the incentive to persevere.

As to the rest of the "Edwards Crew," your obvious loyalty to each other and Mama Toots along with your respect for the Word of God helps me along through each day and provides me with confidence in each of you for the future and beyond. Please continue to stay close to God and to each other. Thank you!

The effort put into writing this book is dedicated to God. Without Him this book would not be possible. Let us allow God to speak directly to each of us through His Holy Word!

RetroClipArt.com

ACKNOWLEDGEMENTS

I wish to express my appreciation for the faithful, tireless counsel, editing, and proof-reading provided by my son "Bo" James B. Edwards II, daughter Judy Clair Turbeville, and my wife Virginia Ann Edwards. Without the support of these three I would still be procrastinating without completing this book.

My wife was sent to me by God. She has provided many years of support and patience. Her thoughts of insight and wisdom are often the seeds of my words written in this book. She is my earthly "guardrail." Her steadfast diligence still holds promise for me, yet.

RetroClipArt.com

Appreciation and respect go to Tony Bosley at RetroClipArt.com for rescuing the images in this book. Additional thanks go to Winifred Rodgers for her editorial refinements.

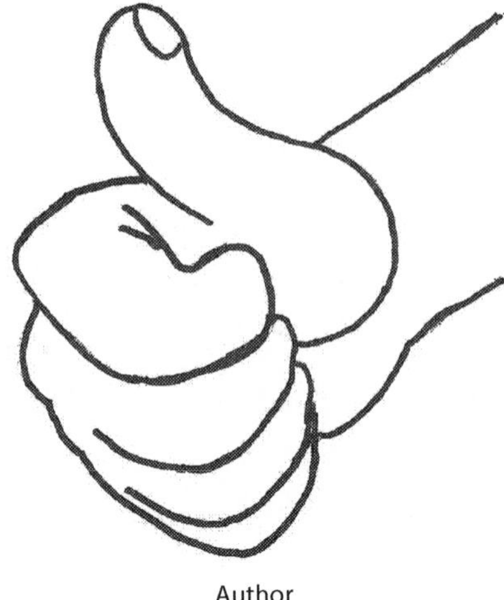

Author

WARNING!

Reading this book may become challenging to your point of view!

It was written solely for those willing to consider a viewpoint other than their own. Perhaps, God's Viewpoint would be preferable.

This is not a "feel good" book for mankind. It is meant only to please God by challenging readers to see reality from God's Point of View. It is not intended to offend anyone but it will likely exasperate some. If that happens you should talk about it with God in prayer.

If you do not believe in God or the Bible then this book may appear to you as noisy confusion ("babel"). Maybe that is reason enough for you to read it as you may discover something that you do not already know that may prove to be critical for your future.

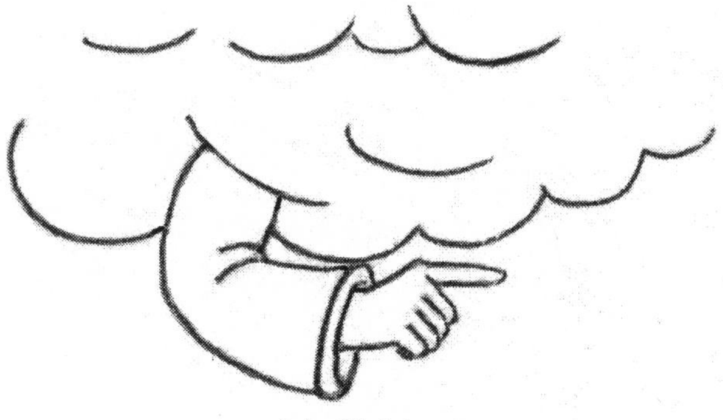

RetroClipArt.com

CONTENTS

The Book Cover xix
Symbols xxi
Meditation xxvii
Preface xxix
Notice of Style xxxi
Introduction xxxv

1. Getting Started 1
2. Purpose 6
3. Who Are We Talking About? 13
4. Foundations 45
5. Another Friend's Admonition 59
6. Change of Direction 62
7. On With It 68
8. The Starting Words 72
9. Are You Expecting Anyone To Believe This? 90
10. A First Cause 95
11. Sound Foundation for Faith 100
12. To Know God 105
13. Preparation for Sessions with God 110
14. Session 1: Who Are You God? 114
15. An Intermission Conversation with Thomas 150
16. Session 2: Who Am I God? 162
17. Closing Words 185
18. Conclusions 195

About the Author 201

THE BOOK COVER

Psalm 19: A psalm of David

"The heavens declare the glory of God; the skies proclaim the work of his hands. Day after day they pour forth speech; night after night they display knowledge. There is no speech or language where their voice is not heard. Their voice goes out into all the earth, their words to the end of the world. In the heavens he has pitched a tent for the sun, which is like a bridgroom coming forth from the pavilion, like a champion rejoicing to run his course. It rises at one end of the heavens and makes its circuit to the other; nothing is hidden from its heat. The law of the Lord is perfect, reviving the soul. The statutes of the Lord are trustworthy, making wise the simple. The precepts of the Lord are right, giving joy to the heart. The commands of the Lord are radiant, giving light to the eyes. The fear of the Lord is pure, enduring forever. The ordiances of the Lord are sure and altogether righteous. They are more precious than gold, than much pure gold; they are sweeter than honey, than honey from the comb. By them is your servant warned; in keeping them there is great reward. Who can discern his errors? Forgive my hidden faults. Keep your servant also from willful sins; may they not rule over me. Then will I be blameless, innocent of great transgression. May the words of my mouth and the meditation of my heart by pleasing in Your sight. O Lord, my Rock and my Redeemer."

Observations: In this psalm, David's steps of meditation take him from creation, through God's Word, through David's own sinfulness, to salvation. In these words of scripture God reveals Himself through nature, which reveals to us His power and our finiteness. We learn about His holiness and our sinfulness. As God reveals Himself through our daily experiences, we learn about His gracious forgiveness and our salvation.

SYMBOLS

RetroClipArt.com

In this book a concentric circle is used as a symbol to represent God. A concentric circle has no beginning and no end. The emanate domain of God is represented by a sphere. A circle is a geometrical two-dimensional object while a sphere exists in a three-dimensional space. The sphere in the context of this book does not represent boundaries or limits. It merely suggests the emanate domain of God as envisioned within a series of never ending concentric circles. The diameters have no limits; they extend through infinity in both directions beyond the point where the human mind is able to comprehend. Therefore, the circumferences for the circles forming the sphere, also, move outward beyond boundaries of human understanding.

A series of concentric circles is the foundational source of a sphere. That is, a sphere is a series of concentric circles placed in a 360 degree array completely surrounding and encompassing the common center of all circles in all outward directions. It is a perfectly round object that forms an outer surface of a completely round ball. The outer surface of the sphere within the current text of this book approaches infinity. Infinity pushes beyond the bounds of human comprehension. The interior area of the sphere represents the totality of everything (the universe and beyond to include the Realms of Heaven.) Within this area the domain of God is represented.

Each concentric circle within the sphere is formed with equal distances from the center to all points; meaning that God is the center of all things and He is omnipotent (He has all power.) {Revelation 11:17} Everything emanates from Him. Each instant of a radius *(r)* in a circle within a sphere begins from God and flows outward. He is the creator of all things (He made everything.) {Revelation 4:11} The diameter traverses across the area connecting opposite edges of the circumference; representing that He is omniscient (He knows everything.) {Psalm 139:2-4} Nothing exists beyond His knowledge and creation. He emanates from the beginning point of the radius, being the center of a circle, and extends in all directions forming the diameters of the sphere. He is the radii. The sphere contains no human recognizable image, representing that God is omnipresent (He is everywhere.) {Psalm 139:8-12, 23-24} He is the Supreme Being that is invisible to the human eye. Yet, we see in the sphere a representation of His invisible qualities (His eternal power and divine nature.) We understand Him from what we have seen in what He has made. We have no excuse. {Romans 1:20}

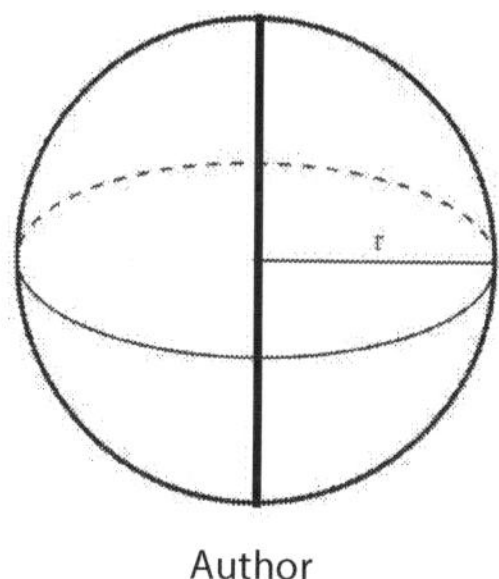

Author

The concentric circle is the metrical composition origin of a sphere. As more concentric circles are added the object eventually results in a full-surfaced ball that is essentially symmetrical and complete.

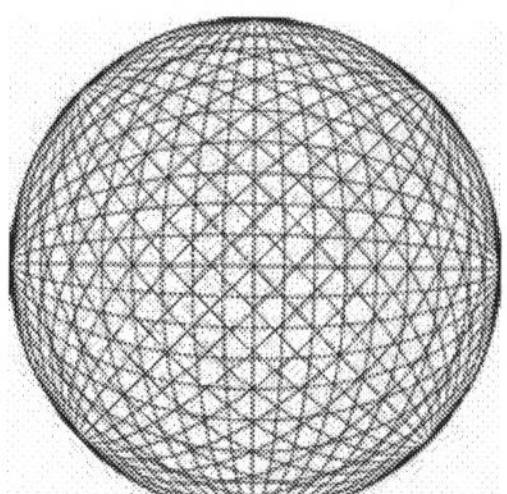

Public domain courtesy of OpenClipArt.org

Below the concentric circle at the top is ∞ which is the symbol for infinity. The infinity symbol is added to represent Eternity. The current instance of time is only momentary. The future stays constantly ahead of us in eternity as the current moment in time quickly becomes the past. We have only been around for a short period of time and we haven't even seen the future yet. God has been and is going to be around for a long time. As Buzz Lightyear[1] says: *"To infinity, and beyond!"*

Notice that the ∞ symbol does have a crossing representing unity with a common intersection for both directions. The infinity symbol suggests that everything is seen by God from the past and the future, both going and coming.

When God is visualized at the apex of a concentric circle anywhere around the surface of a sphere we find the answer to the mystery of beginnings and endings. It is God Himself connecting the circle together at that point. God is the beginning and end. As you roll the sphere (ball) around you find the apex at any point of the moment that is on the top, thus God's power reaches to all points within the entire area of the sphere. The whole thing works like gravity as objects are held by the gravitational pull to the center of the earth, no matter which point of the surface (circumference) happens to reside at the apex.

Just as a concentric circle has no beginning and no end neither does a sphere or ∞. Some say *"what comes around goes around."* God is the alpha and omega (He is eternal.) {Revelation 1:8} The Lord God is the beginning and the end. The words "alpha" and "omega" are the first and last letters of the Greek alphabet. The ∞ symbol simply points to no beginning or end that we are able to understand. But, it's there regardless of what we might think or believe. It simply goes on and on without end. God is the beginning of infinity. He is at the apex of infinity. It begins from Him.

God the Father is the eternal Lord and Ruler of the past, present, and future. Without Him we have nothing that is eternal, nothing that can change our lives, and nothing that can save us from sin. The concentric circle in this book is used to symbolize our Honor for

[1] "Buzz Lightyear" is a fictional character featured in the *Toy Story* movies.

the One who is the beginning and the end of all existence, wisdom, and power.

The four living creatures cited in Revelation 4:8 never stop saying:

"Holy, holy, holy
is the Lord God Almighty,
who was, and is, and is to come."

The cross is, also, important. It symbolizes the Son of God, Jesus Christ, our savior.

The sign of the fish is often used to represent Christians. Jesus called His first Disciples (Peter, Andrew, James, and John who were fishermen by trade) to become *"fishers of men."* {Matthew 4:18-22, Mark 1:16-20}

RetroClipArt.com

MEDITATION

RetroClipArt.com

Dear God: Please grant us some laughter along our way through this book as we move closer to You in obedience, understanding and faith. Laughter seems to help the medicine go down for some of us. Also, it is enjoyable when there are victories. {Psalm 126:2}

As You know, the author wrestled with You throughout the writing of this book. Please make sure that You did not allow him to succeed with his will, but hopefully Your Will prevailed through every word written in this book. Thank you!

Help us to put away our stubbornness and proceed as the

Bereans did by eagerly searching the Scriptures daily to better understand what You are saying to us today. {Acts 17:11} Help us with our obedience even before we understand Your Instructions. Activate our faith as it pleases You as soon as possible. Enable the spirit of our minds to hold forth truth. Prepare us for Your Rescue.

May Your Armor and Power protect us spiritually, mentally, emotionally, physically, and economically. Remove sin from within and from among us without harm or embarrassment. Please forgive us for our sins and heal us all as soon as possible.

Please bless us all this very day. May Your Light shine upon us all, be gracious to us, and grant unto us Your Mercy and Grace.

May Your Will be done in all things as it pleases You. For Yours is the Kingdom, Power and Glory forever and ever. Thank You for Your Love and Patience.

Through the Name of Jesus let us all say "amen." "AMEN!"

PREFACE

This book was written as a result of encouragements by friends of the author in later life. For many years the author has enjoyed chatting with friends and associates on a number of subjects, including Christianity.

Many of these exchanges usually involved some bantering except when the discussion involved Christianity. The subject of Christianity always seemed to take a more serious direction. The author was usually expected to come up with a plausible answer for most questions as he was seldom left out of the question: "What do you think?"

Having been well grounded in Christian faith by his grandparents, who raised him, the author seemed to have more factual answers than others. Also, his answers were usually laced with words in an apt, clever, and amusing way. He is seen to be witty and honest. He uses simple stories, both real and imagined, to illustrate a moral or religious point. He has his own set of parables drawn from his early life experiences of being raised by his grandparents to whom he attributes most of his positions today.

Because of these real life discussions you will find this book to be like the discussions that gave rise to this book. As conversations do wander around somewhat, you will see this book moving about in the same fashion. It unfolds more as a conversation than a well-organized essay or treatise. This is natural for the author, so he makes no claim to following all the rules of formal writing. He just talks to readers through this book.

NOTICE OF STYLE

RetroClipArt.com

This book is not systematic. The author simply writes as his thoughts occur. It is not a treatise. It is a "potpourri." Some portions are written in *conversational style*. This style of communicating is more palatable than formal prose. It is the normal way in which we usually communicate our thoughts to each other.

As conversations often do, some of the topics may be interrupted, then revisited, or continued later. In fact the topic of interruption may get interrupted. This usually happens as a result of some abrupt change in our focus of attention that moves the flow of our thinking to an entirely different subject. Thoughts just pop up in our minds all of a sudden. The current subject simply fades under the arrival of a whole different subject or point that suddenly changes the focus of our attention. It's just the normal way in which we humans usually carryon some conversations.

Where two or more people are engaged in dialogue there may be two or more subject threads running around. The human mind does tend to wander around sometimes, all by itself. Sooner or later, we catch up with our thinking and finally gather it all together. Certainly, the author rambles on occasion, but many of his friends have encouraged him to write it like he tells it to them. Just hang on for the entire journey of this book. Reflection is more enlightened than speculation.

(Attention aspiring writers: Transitions are way overrated.) Often we wander in different directions. We all have our own steps. You can move through this book anyway you chose. You can turn the pages yourself.

There was a sign once that said, *"I know that you think you fully understood every word I said. What you do not understand is that I really did not say what I meant."* [2] It is sometimes difficult to be

---

[2] Talking signs? Yep! See'm all around. Your brain uses your eyes to channel the words right in. Walt Disney enabled us to hear and understand just about everything in sight. Walt brought life right through the vail from "virtual reality" to people.

true unto ourselves. Self-deception can be dangerous for each of us. However, if we keep talking we may eventually find the right words to say what we really mean. Hopefully, we can think our way through the points in this book together and find words that express truth to all of us.

This approach allows the author to say what he thinks at the moment rather than trying to think what to say. This style, also, enables the author and readers to think informally instead of guarding our dialogue. It enables the author to contemplate God's Views. In addition, it allows the author to consider some possible viewpoints of the readers. It's like stepping in three sets of shoes: God's, the author's, and the readers'.

Readers of books always have the power to pause, reflect and think without the continued babbling of the author. Readers can shut the author down anytime they chose. And they can turn the author back on whenever and wherever they determine. This allows readers to think freely from time to time. Reader discernment prevails, which is one of the major goals of this book. Hopefully the discernment comes by way of an objective examination of scripture, relevant facts and applied wisdom.

If you view the author as being arrogant or imposing then you are focusing on the author when you should be listening to God. The author is not attempting to force his understanding of the Word of God on you. Rather, he is encouraging you to allow God to explain His Word to you. If you are unconcerned with operating within the bounds of God's authority, this book will carry no weight of agreement with you.

In all likelihood God said what He meant and meant what He said as He spoke to mankind through the Bible. It seems logical that God would speak to humans using human language when He expects us to understand what He said. For example, the most likely day revealed in the Book of Genesis is the same common 24-hour day we understand today, because God was speaking to mankind for our edification. Why would He confuse us at this point in our relationship with Him?

Throughout this book all references to God are capitalized at the first letter out of respect for His Holiness. God is Sovereign. No one other than God is "reverend." {Psalm 111:9} There are no others before Him and He has no peer. {Exodus 20:3} The practice of presumptuous religious activity means one has asserted himself or herself to the same level as God without the powers of a real god of creation and eternal determination. This seems to be a bit empty-handed and somewhat more naked than Adam and Eve. Satan seems to have traveled this path. After all, Satan tempted Eve and persuaded her and Adam to disobey God.

As an expression of appreciation, all references to Jesus Christ are also capitalized. This practice is not commonly found in many writings. The fact that He is the Son of God, and His sacrifice for each of us, certainly elevates Him far above mortal mankind. He is a Member of the Trinity and He sits on the right-hand side of God in Heaven today. He is entitled to our respect. {Mark 14:62}

INTRODUCTION

In this book, the author shares his experiences and ideas about Christian faith, using personal anecdotes and some third-party stories to illustrate how God works in the lives of the faithful. He explores some of the obligations and responsibilities of Christians and illustrates how to find comfort and guidance in the Bible. Relevant examples are provided throughout the book.

A rational approach is used to develop a "thought-based" comprehension of who God is, who we are, why we are here, and where we go when we leave this place called "earth." Readers are challenged to think about their relationship with God using unique and interesting simulated dialogs between the author, God, and a friend that draw a clearer understanding of the Words of God, and appeal to the reader to recognize that God has the final word on the whereabouts of mankind in eternity.

For those willing to consider God's viewpoint rather than their own, this book seeks critical messages seen as the Final Word of

God. The author builds from some of his life experiences and uses humor to lighten the conversation.

Mysteries such as the purpose and fate of mankind, the Tree of Life and God's Laws of Mathematics are explored. A symbol for God is proposed.

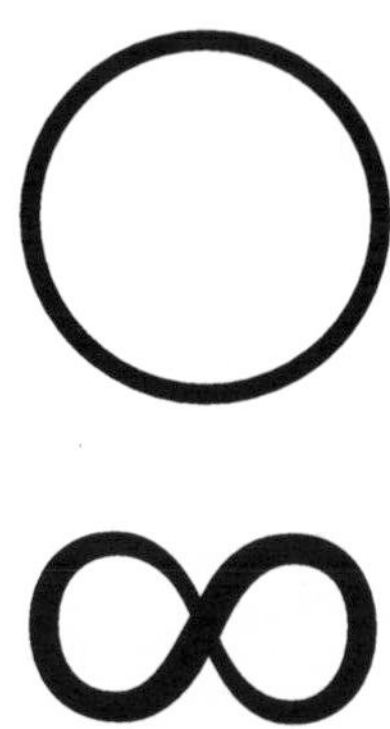

1

GETTING STARTED[3]

RetroClipArt.com

"I'll respond to that!"

[3] Eventually there are beginnings.

You really should not skip to the ending. If you read the ending first you may become confused quicker. Besides you may be disappointed before you get your money's worth. Too, the plot is more revealing as a foldout. If you paid full price for this book you should see it through from the beginning before you waste your money's worth.

In the beginning (most things really do start here) I was just doing some thinking all by myself when a friend, Richard White (Rich), asked me what I was thinking about. It's somewhat hard to think by yourself anymore. You know, with all the noises around like radios, TVs, magazines, newspapers, telephones, car horns, bosses, spouses, parents, and people like my friend Rich who asked me what I was thinking about, etc. (etc. gives you, the reader, a chance to complete the list to your liking) . . . all pushing their commotions and presence into our thinking.

And to think I have to pay for all this media[4] stuff when I buy products. I call it the "media levy" that the advertisers are pushing on us through our purchase prices. Sometimes I confuse the salesperson by requesting a box of their product without the TV charges. I am sure you can visualize the stare I get.

I did get a response once when a salesperson informed me that I could get a $1 coupon that I could apply to a future purchase of the same product if I mailed the box top in to an address on the box. Given the price of postage, this caused me to look at the box with some degree of inquisition. As I was examining the box it

[4] Did the media (radio, TV, magazines or newspapers) ever just report the news? I never have wanted balance from the established sources. Just give me the facts. I want the truth please. Error is already too far in the popular lead, so why do we need fairness to make room for more error. Yes, I realize I just touched some sensitivity buttons. In that case, maybe you should write your own book. This one is mine, thank you!

occurred to me that the producer of the product apparently spent more money for the multi-colored box and advertising than was probably spent for the product in the box that I was purchasing.

O well, so much for that diversion. Now back to my friend's question. When I began to answer the question posed by Rich he interrupted and advised me to write it down.[5]

At first, I thought it was just a way of getting me to hush. But, my friend Rich said, *"no, you should share these thoughts with other people and the best way to do this is to write a book."*

At first, I said, *"you must be kidding."* Then Rich[6] kept asking (pressing) me for several months whether I had written any of this stuff down. I could hardly believe that Rich even remembered that I had ever said anything. Surely, no one listens to me, except to identify my flaws and push corrections on me! I saw my name on a list once and it was not even in alphabetical order. It was more like a "hey you" list.

I usually identify real well with "Hagar the Horrible." He and his sidekick, Lucky Eddie, are vicarious friends of mine. Hagar often feels all alone with his job and problems. He seems so out of touch with his crew. Hagar seems to be a free spirit except for the admonitions of his wife, Helga. And Lucky Eddie resides apart from Hagar in his own world of simple innocence. You don't have to be isolated to feel lonesome. When you are surrounded by a lot of self-focused people, you sure can get to feel this way even in a crowd, just like Hagar.

When you belong to the "skip-generation" you can easily conclude that nothing much ever really comes to us anyway.

---

[5] Rich actually encouraged me to write songs. Everything I said sounded like the name of a new song to him. Apparently Rich did not notice the difference.

[6] Friends are those who give you good advice, aren't they?

Okay, what is the "skip-generation?" Well, it's people in my age range (you don't really need to know the exact range). "So?" Okay! When I was a kid I came last. That is, adults were important. Adults ate at the big table first at church eating meetings and family feast gatherings. Kids ate after the adults had their fill of the best stuff. No problem though. We kids always respected adults and looked forward to the day when we would become one and enjoy the privileges of adulthood.

Then just when I got to be an adult (don't ask me the exact age on this one either) they switched things around the other way. The young'uns ("youth" to those of modern parents) got the privileges and we adults (remember that I am one of those now) became subservient to the young'uns. So I missed out altogether. I am a member of the "skip-generation."

Add being a good citizen, honesty, a desire to work, some reasonable logical sense, relevant education, a willingness to yield and submit for the common good and you done got yourself eliminated from a whole bunch of good stuff. However, that may not be such a bad state to be in, given these times and conditions of uncertainty.

You may be part of a very small group. It could be a group so small (me, myself, and I) that it can meet all together at one time in a phone booth. Then you look around, all of a sudden, to find that all the phone booths have been removed and you are standing all alone. It isn't all bad, though. There may be some privacy found out there somewhere.

RetroClipArt.com

"Endangered Species"

"There's always room for you in the House of the Lord"

RetroClipArt.com

2

PURPOSE

RetroClipArt.com

"I'll just drink on my own, thank you!"[7]

[7] A talking horse? Yep! Walt Disney has a bunch of them talking. You do understand "horse sense" don't you!

The main purpose of this book is to encourage all of us to seek the truth within the Word of God for ourselves directly. It has been said that you can lead a horse to water, but you cannot make the horse drink. By salting the horse's oats the horse could become thirsty and drink voluntarily. By being himself, the author is trying to get and hold your attention in an appeal to you for your objective and independent thinking about God.

Discontent is not an objective of the author in writing this book. Hopefully, you will listen to God and become obedient to Him in all His ways. You should find joy within the protection revealed in the Word of God.

You are entitled to your own opinions, but you cannot change truth. Facts are not alterable. You can make false statements but that does not modify the truth.

In our search for truth we need to avoid creation of a fantasy about what a new object of attention can do for us. We often experience disappointment and dissatisfaction, either real or imagined, as we focus our attention on objects that have no power to rescue us from all the forces and consequences of evil.

Upon reading this book, you need only to search for God's truth and act accordingly as God reveals it to you directly through His Word. His Word is Truth. {John 17:17} His sovereignty makes His Word the Final Word. {Revelations 11:17} We must learn to live by every Word that proceeds out of the mouth of God. {Matthew 4:4} We need to do this without fear with a smile on our face as faithful, believing, knowledgeable, obedient, forgiven sinners. When you know the truth and practice it you will become free. {John 8:32}

Life's Experiences

The author is taking the same journey along with each reader as some of the issues of life and death are studied in this book. Readers should contemplate their own experiences as the author shares some of his. Your experiences are better known to you than the author's. Certainly, they are more relevant to you.

Always let your mind think on those experiences most familiar to you as you observe those of the author. It is okay to dismiss the author's experiences and replace them with your own. But you will need to consider how God may view your experiences and your reactions.

Please view the frankness and levity in this book as an attempt to put a little salt in your oats so that you may come to drink the Word of God on your own. Sometimes a bit of levity helps us relax and listen more clearly.

Submission to God is Plain and Simple

Obedience to God is the desired outcome as a result of thinking through this book. A stronger faith usually takes a little longer to happen.

The development of our understanding happens continuously throughout life on earth. Trust comes through understanding. So please let your understanding develop as you think through this book.

Faith and obedience should improve as you respond objectively to your understanding of what God has to say as you think through this book. God has declared that obedience is better than sacrifice. {First Samuel 15:22} Obedience is the product of our love for

God. {John 14:21} Our love for God develops as we increase our understanding of Him.

God's love for us is shown, first, in creation and, second, in our salvation. Our love for God is shown in our responses to His Will.

Our access to learning the Will of God is provided in the Bible. Our trust in God is demonstrated by our faith in God as we understand His Words and follow His Will in our lives on earth. We simply cannot translate God's Directives to accommodate our preferences.

Problem Solved

Jesus became the only perfect sacrifice and suffered on the cross for our sins. Not even death could stand in His way. He has the power of life over death energized by love from God.

Sin separated us from life in the immediate presence of God {Ephesians 4:18 and Isaiah 59:1-2} and brought death into the world. {Romans 5:12} Jesus destroyed death and brought life with God and immortality to light. {Second Timothy 1:10}

Jesus' death on the cross was a very high cost of delivering us from sin. God required a perfect sacrifice for our sins. Only Jesus could pay that price because He was without blemish or defect. {First Peter 1:19} He paid it all. He took away our sins. {First John 3:5} He destroyed the works of the devil. {First John 3:8}

Jesus entered heaven and appeared before God for us as our High Priest. {Hebrews 9:24} We now have access to God through Christ who intercedes for us. {Romans 8:34} He speaks to God in our defense. {First John 2:1-2} As a result we need not fear death. {Hebrews 2:14-15}

During Our Time

We must understand that mercy and grace happen effectively only during our lifetime on earth rather than afterward. It is not a postmortem occurrence. Upon the death of our bodies we move into the evaluation phase of our lives as human beings where we will be judged by Jesus. {John 5:22}

Our access to mercy, grace, and the new life takes place when we are buried with Christ through baptism into His death, not ours. The mercy of God comes through the sacrifice of Jesus for our sins as they are forgiven through the blood of Christ. Our new life is a gift of grace by God. We rise from baptism to begin a new life here on earth as forgiven sinners. {Romans 6:3-4} We walk in this newness of life. {Romans 6:34} We no longer offer our bodies to sin. Sin is no longer our master. {Romans 6:6-14}

We allow the Holy Spirit control over our carnal bodies so that we become as Teflon to sins. We are not removed from the presence of sin here on earth, but we are protected from it. {Romans 8:9-17}

Response Tone

The natural response to such free grace provided for us is a love that generates a spontaneous praise from our hearts and a submissive commitment to God. God's mercy extended to us was costly. He brought, through purchase, us back into His presence by sacrificing the blood (the essence of life) of His Son, Jesus. {Ephesians 1:13-14}

Love shapes our obedience to God. Without love we are *"only a resounding gong or a clanging cymbal."* {First Corinthians 13:1} When choosing a gift for someone we love, we should give them what they need instead of what we want them to have.

The bridge for our obedience to God is built upon an understanding of His Special Language of Love instead of a language of legalese while seeking "loopholes." We still must adhere to His Directions but with an attitude of a desire to do so. We must do the right things for the right reasons.

God is not an enforcer of the conduct of our behavior. He does not force us to do right. He has spent the entire lifetime of mankind urging us to do the right things for the right reasons according to His wisdom and satisfaction. But He does not judge us. He gave all judgment to Christ. {John 5:22} Each one will receive what is due him for things done while in the body, whether good or bad. {Matthew 16:27 and Second Corinthians 5:10}

God does not make us listen. We have to do this for ourselves. Ignorance may be an excuse, but it is not a solution. Many of us dismiss information we don't understand without trying to discover what it means and its' relevance to us. A study by one of the top business consulting firms (Deloitte, 2016) of major business executives revealed that 96% of business executives discount data[8] they don't understand. This reminds one of the ostrich with its head buried in the sand. Maybe the ostrich needs some thirst inducing salt along with the horse.[9]

---

[8] The word "data" comes from the Latin word "datum," which means "raw facts." In order for data to become "information" it must be transformed into meaningful understandings that are usable.

[9] Or instead of the horse as the horse is known to have some sense.

RetroClipArt.com

"Who turned out the light?"

3

WHO ARE WE TALKING ABOUT?

RetroClipArt.com

Before we dwell further into the pages of this book, maybe we all need to examine ourselves so that we are not always talking about someone else. This book is meant to be about you and me and our relationship with God. Those other people we often tend to talk about should read this book for themselves.

Do you have any idea who you really are? Do you have a clue as to what drives you to do the things you do? Say the things you say? Do you even recognize your own thinking? Are you the person you need to be? Are you really pleased with yourself? Are you sure that God is pleased with you? Do you realize how you appear to an "all-seeing" God? Do you even know how to find out what God may think about you and all the others who are like you?

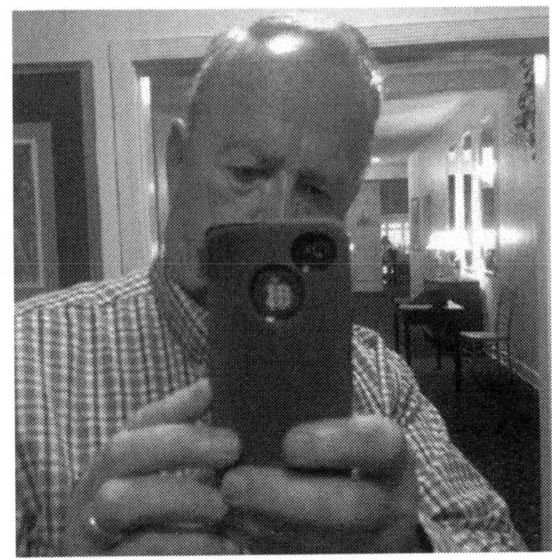

Author

"Is that selfie really me?"

When Does Maturity Happen?

The whole thing about life is really growing up, making decisions independently, and doing the right things for the right reasons. There was a young man who upon leaving home to pursue his adulthood chose to make about every mistake one can make as an immature young man without becoming incarcerated. When asked why he was doing this, he replied *"my parents have exercised absolute control over me all of my life unto now. Now I'm showing them they can't tell me what to do anymore."*

That young man had not yet achieved freedom from the influence of his parents. His behavior was still derived from the moving (to cause to do or say) of his parents. The results were, surely, not those desired by his parents. Never the less, he had not yet considered the alternatives and chosen what is best for one's self. He is now a person held captive by his lack of wisdom and self-determination. He has not achieved independence or the freedom he thinks he has gained.

Life Styles

RetroClipArt.com

"Wait just a minute, and I will help you!"

Let's turn from that young man and examine ourselves. It never helps us to beat up on other people, especially when we have some things to fix ourselves. We can help others after we help ourselves. That is not being selfish. It's more like the instructions given on a commercial airplane where you are told to secure your oxygen mask before you help a child with their mask. You must become safe and stable yourself before you affect others. {Matthew 7:3-5}

Some of us are set in life styles in which we are comfortable but do not conform to the choices of others or those of God. We may be so self-centered and independent that we expect everything around us to conform to our way of satisfaction. However, it is unrealistic to expect this to happen. We can't expect others to depart from their zones of independence and comfort to join ours. Certainly, God did not form His Word to conform to our life style. We just do not have this kind of power or influence. This can isolate us apart from other people and from God.

RetroClipArt.com

"My VIP list."

Disagreeable

"No, no, . . . no, I do not agree!"

RetroClipArt.com

"You are wrong!"

Some of us just want to fight with anybody. We may carry a chip around on our shoulder just looking for someone to disagree with. Reminds me of a boyhood acquaintance who loved to fight so much that when he came upon a brawl he would inquire if it was private or was it open to anyone to join the fight. He did not care about taking a side. He would engage in a slug-fest with whoever appeared in his view.

Many of us do not choose to fight physically, but we can really punch hard with words. We may simply live a good bit of our lives in opposition to most anyone encountered. We may listen to others only to find a target to attack. In this condition, we could become "unreachable" since we are hunters. We do not allow input. No one else matters. We may close the door with, both, God and Satan. We often take contrary positions within ourselves as if to avoid joining any alliance. This creates divisions in which we become an island unto ourselves. We reign over an "isolated" empire.

Some of us will pour gas on top of ourselves and light the match to heap fire on ourselves. Our conscience thoughts become mere figments of our imagination, resulting in an unreal world for ourselves. Reminds me of the fella who had over indulged in drinking the "liquid spirits" at "happy hour." The next day he was charged with setting a hotel on fire during the night. He responded to the judge: *"Your honor, that bed was on fire when I got into it."*

Go With the Flow

RetroClipArt.com

"Hey guys, I am with you!"

Sometimes we may go with the prevailing "political correctness" within our environment. Unwittingly, we are held "hostage" to people and circumstances around us. We are submerged into the local "status quo" as a volunteer. Eventually, we are left to sink or swim on our own when we can no longer ride the tide. The down draft of the current swallows us whole. We are left without a sense of the best direction to take whether on land, on the sea or in the air. We are abandoned by the objects of our loyalties. Unwittingly, we become the prey as our allies turn on us. We must realize that "political correctness" emanates from a perspective that is based on human preferences rather than God's will for us. Truth is not the result of a majority vote cast by humans. The person who sees things from a "heavenly perspective" does not view earth as their home. Life on earth is just a place one is passing through on a journey where heaven is the final destination. One should not get stuck in any stops along the route to heaven.

God really made this one clear in Colossians 2:8 when He said *"See to it that no one takes you captive through hollow and deceptive philosophy, which depends on human tradition and the basic principles of this world rather than on Christ."*

Dependencies

Author

"I'm Okay!"

Some of us never grow up. We simply ride through life freely on the transportation of others. We expect that someone else will provide for our needs. Some other person must clean up our messes. We never take responsibility for anything. We tend to ignore rules and override the rights of others. We consider ourselves predestined to enjoy entitlements not belonging to us. We take without giving or contributing. No one else is of any importance.[10] We get in front of the line for all benefits. We never pick up the check at a café. I once had such a person actually take food from my hand-held plate rather than visiting the buffet for themselves at a reception.

Addictions

RetroClipArt.com

Some of us are held hostage by substance abuse. We seek relief from life's woes through artificial means of relief and comfort. These addictions take over our lives along with our financial resources. We think that we can always walk away from these attractions. But in the meantime we are always taking just one more dose. The temptation of the lure is too attractive.

[10] Our noses tend to extend above our foreheads in the presence of others.

Targets

RetroClipArt.com

"I worked hard for that!"

We may be so focused on our careers and obtaining money that we seldom think of much of anything else. There's nothing wrong with wealth itself. The Old Testament is filled with men of considerable wealth who did not appear to worship wealth such as Abraham, Job, Solomon, David and many others. In the New Testament, First Timothy 6:17 reveals that God giveth us richly all things to enjoy. The rich in the world are charged to trust in God rather than uncertain riches. They are warned by God not to be high minded. Wealth has the power to deceive us into thinking that money is the answer to all our needs. In the second prayer cited in Psalms 119, in verse 14, the speaker of the prayer says, *"I have rejoiced in your laws as much as in riches."* For those of us who are less endowed with earthly possessions, we should not covet {Romans 13:9} what is not ours, regardless of how someone else obtained that which we wish for. We should not even envy or be jealous of what others have. It is dangerous. {Romans: 13:12-14}

Compromise

RetroClipArt.com

"Okay, you can have the rope!"

Many of us are too willing to compromise many important issues. While there are situations where surrendering some portion of our position can be partially gainful, there may be cases where we are merely minimizing our losses. In this case we still sustain some loss. A view can be postulated that when one insists on comprising, that person is not getting what they want, so they are making sure that no one else gets what they want either. "Give and take" negotiations often leave everyone without something.

Visualize two people standing on opposite sides of a river insisting that the other person come on over to their side. Finally, as if to solve anything, they agree to meet in the middle of the river and thereby they both are swept down the river together to some place that is not desirable by either person. In some cases a comprise results in one party getting part of their desire while the other loses a part of their desire. In this case compromise creates an imperfect winner and an absolute loser. The loser gets nothing and the winner is less than satisfied, which results in creating two losers to some extent. Truth does not comprise on anything. There are no half-truths. There may be parts that are true while some are false, but together they do not represent a whole truth.

Make a Deliberate Decision

RetroClipArt.com

"I'm just not certain about that!"

Some of us are just not sure about the future and find it difficult to make a decision. The late Yogi Berra[11] once said *"The future ain't what it used to be."*

There are not many guarantees in life on earth. Because of this some of us can't decide on much of anything. We have no convictions. We either follow the crowd or, simply, watch everything from a distance.

---

[11] Yogi Berra is a former baseball catcher for the New York Yankees. He is deceased.

RetroClipArt.com

Some of us will get in a longer service line when there are obvious shorter lines available. Once asked why this person made such choices, he answered *"because it is a more popular choice, it must be better."* Some of us don't get in any line at all. As a stand-off person I might say *"I am afraid to make a mistake."*

We are like sheep without a shepherd. We may go astray aimlessly. We cannot seem to recognize the best "Pied Piper." We may flow with the "tune of the moment" or we may simply wander through life with no sense of real direction at all. Sometime we feel safer in this condition.

RetroClipArt.com

Some of us will not get in any line. We are comfortable with our current state of being. Some call this "independence." But it may result in isolation from all forms of human fellowship.

Of course, some of our decisions are not good when they are not well thought out. It could be observed that many good decisions are made during bad times while many bad decisions are made during good times. The incentives are different. Else, how or why do we move among conditions? These are not always the best of times, especially when we have not allowed our minds to discover and examine the truths before us that affect us.

Cheated

RetroClipArt.com

"That's not fair!"

Sometimes we feel that other people have things that they do not deserve. Or, at least, we feel that we deserve them too, but do not have them. Among our fellow mankind we feel "cheated" and believe that others should not have some things either. Reminds me of the time Charlie asked Sam for a $4 loan. Sam handed Charlie $2. Sam retorted that this was $2 short. Sam simply replied that it was fair that each of them lose $2 because he felt that Charlie would never repay the loan.

My favorite on this point is the dog in a manger story. The dog sees the horses and cows enjoying eating the hay and thinks that he should have the same enjoyment too. After a disappointing tasting of the hay the dog begins to bark so loudly that the horses and cows are distracted from eating. So the dog prevents anyone else from enjoying the hay just because it is not enjoyable for the dog.

The saddest case is where one feels that by being a Christian they must sacrifice too much in their life on earth. They see others, seemingly, enjoying activities that God does not approve of. Yet, they feel cheated by the life-style prohibitions of God, especially when they learn that God can forgive others for things they should not have done. They may be looking through the wrong end of a telescope at the gates to Heaven. They may not have focused in on the fact that God is guiding us to what is in our own best interest.

Parity does not seem to be a natural law of life on earth, but we are promised that someday we will be rewarded according to what we have done on earth. {Revelation 22:12} For those that do the right thing on earth they can look forward to better things later. But we need to be careful with this way of thinking as we cannot change our destiny after death or if we face Christ sooner. {Revelation 22:11} The clock is ticking our lifetime away. Instead of feeling left out we need to focus on understanding and doing the right things within this life.

Left Out

RetroClipArt.com

"Home alone!"

Sometimes we find ourselves crying out to God without finding Him. We feel all alone. We may be stretching empty arms heavenward experiencing troubling thoughts about God because of horrible circumstances, enduring unspeakable trouble. We may be cowering under the feeling of being cast aside, fearing failed promises and expectations, even fearing a lack of sufficient mercy. Yet God is very much aware of us. Even the number of hairs on our head is known by Him. {Matthew 10:30}

Isolation

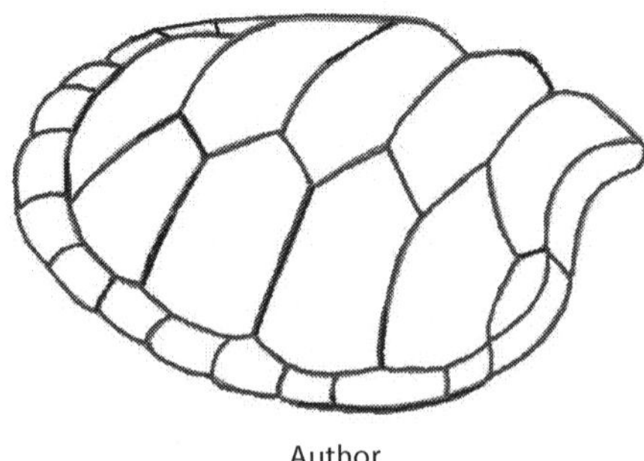

Author

"I'll just stay here safely in my shell."

Some of us choose to be alone. We simply drop out of everything and sequester in our isolated confines. We do not maintain family relationships. We have no friends. We live innately. We perform our jobs as if we were robots programed to do what we do each day without variation. Our jobs tend to be more procedural rather than behavioral. Employment is nothing more than a source of subsistence. No one is expected to do anything for us and we do not feel compelled to interact with anyone beyond minimal necessary transactions.

The fatal part comes when we shut God completely out of our lives. We do not allow Him to use others to help us with anything and we do not serve others either. So we are insulated within our cocoon from hope for anything more than the domain of our reclusive shell.

The Blame Game

RetroClipArt.com

"Don't point at me!"

While we claim to know God, we may blame Him for some of the misfortunes in our lives. We see our infirmities as coming from God, being inflicted upon our innocence. We fail to understand the effect of sin on mankind as a whole. We need to understand all the forces affecting our lives.

This may be one of the most dangerous situations to be in. It can lead to a hardness of the heart as one turns their back on God; thus, rejecting faith in God. According to Matthew 12:30-32, we may lose access to God's forgiveness for the sins we have committed.

Can You Hear?

RetroClipArt.com

"You said something?"

In his book *The Problem of Pain*, C.S. Lewis observed that *"God whispers to us in our pleasures, speaks in our conscience, but shouts in our pains: it is His megaphone to rouse a deaf world."* Sometimes we need to shift our thinking from immediate circumstances so that we can listen to God. In the tenth prayer cited in Psalms 119, in verse 75, the speaker of the prayer says, *"I know, O Lord, that Your judgements are right, and that in faithfulness You have afflicted me."* Do you hear God at all?

Experiences in life can be a painful teacher. But some preventive education can be much less painful. By studying the Bible in advance we can avoid some unpleasant experiences in life and, perhaps, eternity. As long as we are alive we always have an opportunity to know and to do better.

Too Late

RetroClipArt.com

"Don't miss the bus!"

Then there are those who feel that it is too late to change. They seem to feel that the bus left without them. There are sayings in many languages about the difficulty of changing long-established habits. In English, *"You can't teach an old dog a new trick."* In Spanish, *"El loro viejo no aprende a hablar"* (An old parrot can't learn to speak). In French, *"Ce n'est pas ă un vieux singe qu'on apprend ă faire la grimace"* (You can't teach an old monkey how to pull a funny face).

As long as we can see a sunrise follow a sunset we can see a new day before us in which we may still, yet, try something different with our lives. It is when our view fades out that we can no longer see a better day in which to become what we need to be. It only takes a moment of understanding for us to change our faith to the truth and respond to God.

Fail Unsafe

RetroClipArt.com

"I make my own proclamations!"

Many of us insist on sovereignty. That is, no one can tell us what to do, including God. Perhaps, this was Lucifer's failure when he lost his job in Heaven. He mistakenly thought that he controlled destiny for himself. He founded a failed kingdom with his fallen angels. His kingdom will perish.

- Have you built some sort of kingdom or empire for yourself?
- Just how powerful is your empire?
- Do you have the power to overcome death?
- How long will your empire last?
- How powerful are your enemies?
- Does your empire have any reliable alliances?
- Do you have a backup plan?
- Do you have an inexhaustible supply of energy to power and protect your empire?

God on Puppet Strings

RetroClipArt.com

"Are you really that powerful?"

Some of us seem to act as if we have God as a puppet on strings. We see God providing us with things to make us happy. We may believe that God provides us with what we desire regardless of what we really need. I have heard some say, *"God just wants us to be happy."* Maybe so, but He will do it His Way to His Pleasure.

Some worship services are very lively with features that make us feel very good about ourselves. There is a sense of gratification. Entertaining services do tend to attract large numbers of joyful people. We really seem to have a good time when we assemble for these wonderful feeling services. On these occasions we seem to be content with our opinion of our relationship with God.

I cannot question the motives of others who enjoy great

performances. God knows whether we are focused on Him rather than ourselves. We may not see ourselves as God sees us. Our joy may not be a joy unto God. But that is for God to determine.

Do You Like Yourself?

RetroClipArt.com

"Are you satisfied?"

Many of us do not feel good about much of anything. Rather than despair, we simply do not find contentment with anything. We try many things for a while, then lay them aside and move on to something else. Sometimes we just do not like ourselves. Dr. Seuss[12] expressed this sadness in the lyrics of his children's book, *Green Eggs and Ham*. His character, Sam did not like "green eggs and ham" and he was not happy with himself as he said:

---

[12] Dr. Seuss (1904-1991) was an American writer and cartoonist best known for his collection of children's books. *The Cat in the Hat* and *Green Eggs and Ham* are classics. Many of his sayings are popular quotes today.

"I am Sam"
"Sam I am"
"That Sam-I-am"
"I do not like that Sam-I-am"

Hopefully, in the style of Dr. Seuss we could say:

"I am me"
"Me I am"
"That me-I-am"
"I do like that me-I-am"

"My soul is here to stay"
"Me-I-am will never go away"
"My soul will always be somewhere, I say"
"I hope me-I-am does not stray from the way I need to stay"

"I hope that God never throws me away"
"I hope that God likes that me-I-am everyday"
"I hope God takes me-I-am to His Place to stay someday"
"I do not like that other place for me-I-am to stay"

"While me-I-am is still here on earth today"
"I hope that me-I-am does not lose sight of that Place me-I-am hopes to stay someday"
"Me-I-am does not want to sway along the way"
"Me-I-am would not want any other place to stay"

"God has prepared the Place me-I-am would like to stay someday"
"I would not like to turn down God's invitation to stay at His Place for me-I-am to stay someday"
"I would not like for me-I-am to turn the other way"
"I would like me-I-am much better if I would not stray some other way"

"I know that I need protection for Me-I-am every day"
"I cannot make it alone with me-I-am all the way"
"I do know that God cares for me-I-am every day"
"I do like me-I-am who God has rescued along the way"

It is highly probable that we are not who we should be if we do not like ourselves. The evils that make man "unclean" come out of man's heart. Matthew 15:18-20 and Mark 7:21-23 states this clearly. That which defiles us begins from within ourselves. Ultimately, we need God to like us, too.

Invisible

RetroClipArt.com

"Are you really invisible?"

Sometimes, many of us think we are hiding from God. Adam and Eve chose to hide from God when they realized that they had disobeyed Him. Yet we cannot hide from God. He knows exactly where we are. In reality, we actually hide God from ourselves so that we cannot see or hear Him. To play "hide and seek" by only hiding without seeking is only "half a game" in life. In the end we will become aware that we were not hid at all. Rather than hide in fear, we need to come out of hiding and respond in this way: *"God be merciful to me a sinner!"* {Luke 18:13} *"Please help me to understand, trust, and obey."*

Good Sense

RetroClipArt.com

"I'll find it!"

Until our thoughts and actions become independent of everyone else we cannot claim to be a person of our own will, much less the Will of God. Good sense is better than common sense. Much of common sense has become bad sense. It is never stable. It is like the flow of water ever seeking a lower-level hole in which to fall. Nonsense has apparently taken the lead over common sense in the popular majority vote count in this world.

"Political correctness" has taken precedence over freedom and liberty; perhaps, God. If we could only locate the chairperson of "they say" and eliminate their power we could remove this harness that holds us in bondage. The truth is what sets mankind free. {John 8:32} And ultimate truth comes from God.

Unreal

RetroClipArt.com

"I saw it myself!"

Illusion and misdirection seems to lead many of us through various episodes in our lives. It is our own reality show. It's like watching an old Three Stooges episode and you think: Okay, I know Larry is going to pivot and accidently hit Moe in the head with that 2-by-4. Then Moe is going to blame Curly and hit him in the head with a mallet. Then they're all going to walk into the kitchen to bake a cake, except Curly is going to confuse the baking flour with the TNT powder and they're going to blow up the house. But it's going to appear funny because we know there's no real harm inflicted. It's all theatrical illusion and we don't blame any of them because their misdirection consequences are not real.

The Three Stooges are acting as uninformed people. But when we experience similar events it is not an illusion and often it means that we have taken a real step in the wrong direction. And the consequences cannot be dismissed with the word "cut" by a producer or laughed off.

Just maybe we dismiss too many happenings with a laugh as we do with the Three Stooges. Recall the "funny bone" comment we all make sometimes when we hit our elbow on something that results in non-fatal pain. The Three Stooges episodes are an exaggeration of some of the similar things that happen to us. It sort of bonds us with Larry, Moe and Curly. It is an obvious trait in mankind to laugh off these episodes as we see others in ways that make us aware of our own imperfections as human beings.

Our "me too" association makes it seem okay, when in fact it is not okay, when it becomes reality. The danger lies in the fact that while the Three Stooges are acting and walk away from the filming set unharmed, we suffer real consequences in our real life episodes. Humor will not resolve our misdirection errors when those errors come as a result of simply being uninformed.

Safe Steps

RetroClipArt.com

"Oops!"

Given obvious poor consequences here on earth in this life should cause us to seek something better. Even without God we need not ever do anything during our life-time that will harm us or that cannot be corrected, fixed, or reversed. Temporal (earthly) consequences are bad enough, so why risk the eternal ones when you can know what they are from the Word of God.

Most of us need a changed perspective. We should not allow ourselves to be defined by our failures. While we can't always control the things of life that impact our lives, we do have a chance to see things in a truer relationship (good and bad.) We can continue to allow the "mess-in-our-lives" to shape who we really are, or we can change our perspective. We need not brood over things. We really need some help in surviving carnal life. We need to be guided by the Promises of God.

Sadly, some people just don't care about their soul! Since they can't see it, it's easy to forget about it or place little to no value on it. Then death arrives, as it always does. Suddenly, people may care about their soul during the last moments of their lives as they become concerned about what will happen. For some, there is no time left for them to take the correct steps for salvation. It may be too late for deliverance (redemption) from sin and its effects. It may be said "that we should make hay while the sun still shines."

Look for Hope

RetroClipArt.com

"Help is near!"

Still, we may be frustrated with just about everything. Despair is real and answers do not come easily to some of us. True, there is much to be frustrated about, but many survivors follow the "light of hope" as it springs forth through revealed truth and logic. Survivors seem to have escaped darkness and understand God's glory, majesty, power, and love. Hope is usually built upon some foundation whether well-grounded or not. We need to make sure that our foundation is sound or our hope may never happen.

Have You Noticed the Work of God in Your Life?

RetroClipArt.com

"Did you see the hand of God?"

Some have failed to recognize God's love acting within our lives. We may not have become convicted of God's Power to deal with our requests of Him. I had a recent experience that has had a profound impact on my life.

During a routine checkup with my family physician a murmur was detected in my heart. A visit with the ultrasound machine determined that I had aortic stenosis. I had nine visits with this machine over a three-year period in which the readings were moderate. Then the tenth visit with this machine showed that I had gone from moderate to serious stenosis within four months. Obviously, my cardiologist determined that it was time to open up my heart and replace the aortic value.

Before he was to turn me over to the surgeon, my cardiologist

(Dr. Hollins) decided to perform a heart catheterization and check things out. I talked to God all day long on the day preceding the doctor's visit into my heart area. Finally, just before I went to sleep that night I decided on a simple prayer: *"God, I am prepared to accept whatever happens. But I would like for the doctor to find something to fix that would prevent the need for the valve replacement surgery."* I had taken this position of belief several days earlier and expressed it to some of my friends and family. Now, I expressed it to God.

I slept very little that night. The next morning I was nervous all the way to my turn in the clean room. However, I must say that I never doubted that the doctor would find something to fix. The body was nervous, not my conviction. This was the first time in my life (now eighty years old) that I had ever really felt this convicted that God would make my request happen. This feeling began on the day that preceded the day of the catheterization and continued as the doctor leaned over me as I still lay on the table, with his mask still on, and told me he had good news for me. He said, *"You don't need a new valve. The ultrasound machine exaggerated your numbers. They were all wrong. Your numbers are about the same as three years ago. You still have moderate aortic stenosis. You may need a new valve when you become eighty-five-years old."*

I joyously said, *"Thank you God!"* with Dr. Hollins still right over me. And I still can't seem to stop saying it.

Later, Dr. Hollins kneeled before my wife in the waiting room and humbly told her the good news. In my opinion, that is a doctor on loan from God.

It is amazing how God works things out for us. God knew the ultrasound machine needed fixing and He let it be known. He had already granted my request before the doctor found the real problem.

Then I wondered why God had allowed this to happen in my life. My devotion on the morning of the catheterization focused on John 15:1-11. The vinedresser, God, was pruning me, just as was the case with Saul on the road to Damascus when Saul needed some redirection in his life. The word "abide" appears ten times in these verses. This caused me to realize that I do not always abide in the branches that connect through Jesus to God. I needed to refocus my mind on God.

But the story does not end here. Almost exactly one year later the ultra sound machine issued another warning. This time (now eighty-one years old) the heart catheterization proved the ultra sound machine to be correct. It only took the surgeon (Dr. Tribble) 2½ hours to replace my aortic value and now I have better blood flow and some new found leg strength. This surgery can take several more hours but I know even more that my surgeon and my neurologist were on loan from God because everything went perfect and I can now look forward to a better quality of life. God extended my pruning according to His Will rather than mine.

If you have not had such an experience as this, you need to work on your understanding of *Who God Is* and how you should relate to Him yourself. It has taken me eighty-one years to reach this point in my life. Maybe, some of you could get there sooner than me. Hopefully, your "attention getting" event will be milder than mine.

A living God offers the only promise of anything good beyond life in this temporal world. Why not go for it! Take Him up on His Terms. Trust Him. Smile and be happy as you learn and follow His Word. His Promises will not fail you. Please think through the rest of this book with me as we both strive to find eternal truth. God help us to abide by it when we find it.

4

FOUNDATIONS

RetroClipArt.com

The verbs *"founder"* and *"flounder"* are often confused. *"Founder"* comes from a Latin word meaning *"bottom"* (as in *"foundation"*) and originally referred to a ship's sinking. Today *"foundation"* is known as the basis on which a thing stands, is founded, or is supported. *"Flounder"* means *"to move clumsily, thrash about"* and hence *"to proceed in confusion."*[13] Some of us have floundered through life to

[13] The American Heritage Dictionary, 2nd College Edition, 1991, Houghton Mifflin Company, p 528.

our present condition of thinking. We may become confused by a mixture of our ancestral heritage and changing environmental influences, especially as we move into early adulthood.

Most likely, though, our behaviors have developed through our senses rather than our minds. That is, we settle into zones of comfort where threats are low. Our environments are more likely to eventually influence our behavioral phenotypes than genetic transmissions from our parents. Since our early environments in life are usually dominated by parents we may confuse these formulating experiences with genetics rather than social settings. Moreover, it is our personal social environment that stimulates and develops our mental and moral growth. We likely take on the thinking characteristics of whoever surrounds us during our formative years. However, these formative years may extend into early adulthood as we seek independence from our past.

Some people refer to this phase of our lives as the foundation training period of our lives. It is the girding that prepares us for future decisions and actions in our lives. However, this may not be the same for everyone. I can only share with you my experiences.

My real foundation came from my grandfather ("Papa Jim") and grandmother ("Mama Artie"). My birth father took up drinking too soon in my life, so Papa Jim and Mama Artie fetched me at the age of two and proceeded to prepare me for later service in the U.S. Marine Reserves. They did a good job, as Marine training seemed to be like a vacation more akin to being "at ease" most of the time compared to my home training. Discipline at home ranked above the level of corporal punishment. It was comparable to the drill sergeant level of intensity and it was effective. It was real solid love. It was like heat refining iron ore into steel. I am a much better man as a result of tough love administered by someone who really loved me.

Moses, on behalf of God, covered it well when he wrote in Deuteronomy 8:5, *"Know then in your heart that as a man disciplines his son, so the Lord your God disciplines you."*

Daily chores like taking out the ashes from the fireplaces and the stoves and bringing in wood and coal was considered my work[14] for earning 10 cents ($00.10) per day unless I took the day off from my duties . . . which was treated as an uncompensated absence. (There were no gratuitous allowances.)

Papa Jim ran a general store about 12 miles south of the Atlanta airport. He could obtain almost any legitimate product for a customer within a week. He even had a network for the procurement of wild rabbits; which was a favorite breakfast meat at my grandmother's table along with the greatest made from scratch biscuits on earth. My grown uncle came by almost daily to get a sack full; which delighted her. Of course, he ate a few standing there while she was filling his sack from the warmer compartment atop her wood-burning stove.

The telephone number at the store was the vocal number "11" (just to provide you with some perspective on the state of local communications at that time and the prominence of the store in the community at that time.) All telephone calls, including local, went through an operator who would respond when you picked up the receiver and turned the crank, "number please." You told the operator your desired number and the operator connected your phone to that number. There was no dial on the phone and there was no dial tone.

---

[14] I felt more like a tender railroad car, attached behind, and carrying fuel and water for a steam locomotive.

In addition to the store, Papa Jim operated a very active farm with mules (no tractors or other gizmos). I used to harvest oats with a sickle in my hands. Sometimes it took me five minutes or more beyond quitting-time[15] for my fingers to release the grip I had on the sickle handle. I never had to chop cotton, but I busted the middles with a plow pulled by a mule.[16] Have you ever spent the day following the backend of a mule? It can encourage you to consider other viewpoints in life. By the way, my compensation for the farm work was free room and board. My cash pay grade topped out at ten cents per day for normal chores.

Papa Jim purchased a tractor a few days after I left home (more like released) to find easier work (college). He installed some gas heaters, a hot water heater and provided my grandmother with an electric stove in the house. His bond servant (that's me) had earned his freedom and headed out to see what was in the next county without any entrance support for prodigality.

O yes, I did walk one-mile to school even in bad weather and took my lunch with me from home for 12 years. Took some homemade from scratch biscuits, of course, and a sausage patty or two for lunch. Papa Jim prepared the sausage and Mama Artie applied her craft and packaged the sausages between the best use of flour you can imagine. If the *"eat mor chikin"* folks had tasted one of these sausage biscuits they would have the cows and chickens both saying *"eat more sausage biscuits."*

By the way, I could ride my horse "Minnie"[17] anywhere I chose in the area where I grew up. She was born on Papa Jim's farm. Papa

---

[15] This occurred around dark-thirty after the sun went down.

[16] Some of you may have to research "busting the middles" if you want to clear this sentence.

[17] Named after Aunt Minnie Pearl of Grand Ole Opry Fame.

Jim received a lot of pleasure watching me try to train Minnie to be a saddle horse. After several weeks of bumps and bruises (all mine) Papa Jim hooked Minnie up to a very large plow used for breaking ground and worked her until she was sweating. Then he told me to put the saddle on Minnie. Apparently, Minnie chose at that moment to become a riding saddle horse. Henceforth, she was the perfect caretaker of Papa Jim's grandson (me: nicknamed "Bobo" during my home-based foundation days). One day a neighbor told Papa Jim that he saw me and Minnie about five miles away from home. He was thinking that Papa Jim might be concerned. Papa Jim replied to the neighbor that *"Minnie would bring me safely home in time for supper[18] because Minnie knew where the oats would be."* By the way, Minnie was the fastest horse in the county, and she loved to prove it while I barely hung on.

[18] "Supper" was an alias for dinner during that era and in that community.

Author

Minnie, Bobo, and Papa Jim

Any time you want to see a grown man cry, just come on by and ask me to talk about my grandfather, Papa Jim and my grandmother, Mama Artie.

RetroClipArt.com

Papa Jim was as honest as you can get. He must have gotten his wisdom straight from Solomon. He usually got things correct immediately. He often advised that *"there is no education in the second kick of a mule."* My Papa Jim always looked for solutions. When he was asked by a preacher whether the glass was *"half-full or half-empty"* he simply replied: *"Gim'me two glasses then."*

Papa Jim could have negotiated peace all over the world. He managed the mules on his farm very well. His mules always understood his consistent words. The word *"giddyup"* [19] got them started. He never instructed them to *"gee"* [20] when he wanted them to turn left and he never instructed them to *"haw"* [21] when he wanted them to turn right. The word *"whoa"* [22] brought them to

[19] "Giddyup" spoken as one word to a mule means move forward.

[20] "Gee" to a mule means turn to the right side.

[21] "Haw" to a mule means turn to the left side.

[22] "Whoa" completes the vocabulary of a mule as it means to stop. No one in our community was ever able to teach a mule to go backwards. Some horses have been taught to walk backwards, but, to my knowledge, no mules have advanced to that level. You have heard the words "stubborn as a mule" haven't you? Papa Jim used those words occasionally, referring to some folks he knew.

an immediate stop. They all took him at his word. He did not mix words with anyone. Once he was trading for a brand new $900 automobile. He selected a black, four-door, straight-shift, standard model Chevrolet without the extras (heater, clock, and radio; this occurred before auto air-conditioning). He told the salesman he could put on his coat if he got cold, he had a watch, and that he could think for himself instead of listening to some blabber-mouth on the radio. I don't remember the year model of the auto, so I won't guess at it now. Papa Jim taught me to avoid misleading comments. He counted out nine one-hundred dollar bills and handed it to the salesman. The salesman told him that there would be an additional $27 sales tax. Papa Jim reached for his money back. He told the salesman that he was not a man of his word because he said the asking price of the new auto was $900.

You must understand that Papa Jim sold his general store when the State of Georgia placed a sales tax on consumers (his customers). He believed that it was unlawful taxation and too much trouble to keep up with at the store. He claimed that his customers had already paid income taxes on the money when they earned it. He felt the government (he made no distinction between federal and local) was double dipping (double-taxation) and taking too much money from citizens' earnings. (This makes a lot of $cents to me.)

The owner of the dealership chased Papa Jim as we were leaving shouting *"wait Mister Jim I'll take the nine hundred dollars, here's the keys."* Papa Jim drove the new one home and I got to drive the old one over to the fella who was happily buying it from Papa Jim without any sales taxes. It is amazing how "free-trade" can really work for the happiness of somebody.

Mama Artie must have understood why God made her. She was the classical help-mate to Papa Jim that God appears to have intended in the beginning. She never wavered in carrying out her God-given duties in any way whatsoever. Her support of Papa Jim was an example for all-time. She knew who she was in the sight of God and her husband. Her care for me placed such a hold on me that I could never, ever, do anything that would make her ashamed of me.

Then there was my uncle who was one of the finest human beings that God ever made. He made sure that I was safe at all times and supported every activity of my days of youth. His name was Clifford and his nickname to all the community was "Geechie."[23] When my Papa Jim sold the store and the farm was between agricultural seasons, during my high school days, Geechie put me to work at his auto gasoline station. Back in those days we pumped the gas, checked the water and oil levels, and cleaned the customer's windshield. Geechie taught me to do the right things about the customers. He inherited his values from Papa Jim and he made sure that I understood them too. He only took time off from tending his auto gasoline station when I could be there to watch the cash register. When I would come home from college he would have his bags packed ready to hand me the keys to the station. Given the operating hours of the station, I looked forward to more time for myself back at college. But he paid me fairly, so that I could attend college, and he taught me how to manage my money prudently.

I must take the time to tell you about my initial voting experience. Geechie became chairman of the local board of education when I

[23] "Geechie" is normally spelled "Geechee." My uncle, Clifford L. McEachern, got his nickname and spelling from his high school principal (A.M. Bowen) who misunderstood the pronouncing of "McEachern." He heard "McGeechie" and that's the name the principal anointed him with, except he shortened it to "Geechie." The whole community took to it, except his mother, Mama Artie; and later his wife, Martha.

went off to college. My old high school building burned completely to the ground during my freshman year at college. Geechie sent word to me at college that I needed to come home and register to vote as he would need my vote to gain approval of a bond referendum to replace the school building properly. Well, I hitched-hiked[24] home and went to the window at the county court house to register. The lady at the window knew me, as she knew everyone in the county and a bunch of people at the cemetery. She looked at me through the window and asked *"Bobo, what are you doing home from college?"* I told her that I came home to register to vote. Much to my surprise, she replied *"that I was already registered and had voted in a previous election."* Since that time, I have transferred my registration among several precincts over the years, but I have never registered myself, while I continue to vote as a registered voter today. I think that this "shenanigan" represented some of the reasons my uncle felt that he had to make a difference for the good in our community. His unswerving commitment to what is right was another important training phase in my development as a human being.

Jim, why are you telling us all about Papa Jim, Mamma Artie, and your uncle? I thought you were going to share the interview you had with God. Well, I wanted you to understand my value system and where it came from. Too, it reveals my approach and response to God. My grandparents and my uncle taught me some manners and respect. I just didn't want to upset God by bothering Him with any misrepresentations of myself. Earlier I thought my grandfather had taught me "common sense" but now I have discovered that he was not common at all. He was all about honesty and wisdom. He

[24] A common form of public transportation during those days.

used fundamental logic to find his wisdom, rather than "political correctness" or the prevailing common thinking.

Because of my upbringing I will not even agree to disagree with anyone. Even if we disagree we both may be wrong. So we need to use our minds as we seek understanding about the supernatural realms of God and His Covenants. His Covenants are binding and non-negotiable.

We need to be in command of our own soul before it departs from its earthly habitat (human body) passing into the supernatural eternity. Our soul will not be held captive by the natural world at all. It is our spirit along with the Holy Spirit that testifies that Christians are adopted children of God. {Romans 8:12-16}

Recently I read about a private investigator that would knock on a door, show his badge to whoever appeared, and say, *"I guess we don't have to tell you why we're here."* Often times, the person would look stunned and say, *"How did you find out?"* then proceed to describe an undiscovered criminal act they had committed. Writing in *Smithsonian* magazine, Ron Rosenbaum described such a reaction as *"an opening for the primal force of conscience, the telltale heart's internal monologue."* [25]

We all know things about ourselves that no one else knows that seem to haunt us from time to time. These failures, faults, and sins often come back to accuse us again and again, even after we confess them to God, in spite of His forgiveness. The Apostle John wrote on behalf of God, *"By this we know that we are of the truth, and shall assure our hearts before Him. For if our heart condemns us, God is greater than our heart, and knows all things."* {First John 3:19-20} God, who knows everything about us, is greater than our own self-condemnation. It is very logical to me that I do not want to receive

[25] "The Telltale Heart," David McCasland, *Our Daily Bread*, February 5, 2014.

God's condemnation. So I better logic it out while I still have an opportunity to do so.

I am simply trying to share with you what I see as the most plausible positions to take in contemplating the whole of existence and destinies. We exist in a "time-space" that had a beginning and will have an ending for us here on earth. But beyond our "space-in-time" there may be fewer choices, if any, than we have now. Within our "time-space" the past is growing, the future is getting smaller and the present does not stand still, it is moving.

The present is the dividing point between what has happened and what will happen. The coming step into eternity may be difficult and hopeless for some of us. We just really need to play it safe and find a "fail-safe" venue in which to plot our passage into the "hereafter." There is no substitute for time. Only it can do what it does. Time is not recyclable and does not extend. It is not a renewable resource. Time is not replaceable. It is a consumed resource which dissipates in terms of availability to mankind. It does not regenerate. Each moment of time has a singular space within our lifetime on earth.

The Time of Our Lives on Earth

RetroClipArt.com

(Past → Present → Future)

Past is Growing PRESENT is Moving Future is Shrinking
It is impossible to turn back and chase the past!

RetroClipArt.com

Time Will Not Roll Back

Moses prayed to God in Psalm 90:12: *"Teach us to number our days aright, so that we may gain a heart of wisdom."*

RetroClipArt.com

Beginning End

-->

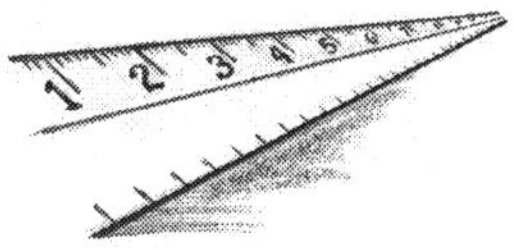

RetroClipArt.com

BIRTH Death

Our Days on Earth are Measured

Observe the Rules of Time on Earth:

- PAST is growing.
- PRESENT is constantly moving.
- FUTURE is shrinking.
- SUBSTITUTE does not exist.
- REPLACEMENTS do not exist.
- AVAILABILITY does not recycle or extend.
- RENEWAL does not happen.

5

ANOTHER FRIEND'S ADMONITION

RetroClipArt.com

"That's what friends do, don't they?"

I was advised by another friend, Jim Redding (JR),[26] to follow the KISS (keep it simple and short) principle. JR thought more people might really read this book if I did not take too much of their time. He probably thinks the previous paragraphs are already beyond the KISS principle. He may be correct.[27]

However, I mostly like to hear and think[28] about things I don't already know, rather than the ninety-ninth rendition of the *"bear went over the mountain to see what he could see."* The bear, over and over, saw another mountain so he continues to go on and on over more and more similar mountains, never seeming to reach a destination or seeing anything new.

Sometimes we need to move forward with prudence and shed things that are not repairable and obtain some new stuff—even our ways of thinking. (I have decided to quit procrastinating on things that I never intend to do anyway.) I recall that I could not walk during my early days on earth, but somehow I improved my dexterity to the point that I could walk on both feet. Believe me when I say that I needed to learn to walk early on in life, mostly to get out of the way. Now I need some additional direction guidance that leads to somewhere rather than nowhere. However I usually do not stay lost very long as my wife often helps me with direction(s).

Okay JR, I know that I am rambling around from point to point and wandering in and out of this conversation. However, that's my style (conversational) and I am sharing my thinking in real-time

---

[26] Some of us are allotted more than one friend, but it is mostly up to us to keep them. Of course, not all my friends claim me as their friend. Being a friend does not always go both ways.

[27] Since this chapter is the shortest chapter I have dedicated it to JR. He should like this one and identify with it.

[28] You are aware that you can talk without thinking, so I am writing instead of talking as a way of sharing my thinking.

as it happens. Gosh, some people can cover several topics and remembrances within a single sentence. I'll bet you think and react the same way. Just hang on to your crayon while we hash out this whole discussion. Maybe you can use your crayon to draw some connecting lines if you need to do so. You could insert a few sentences yourself along the way. (You paid for your copy of this book, didn't you?)

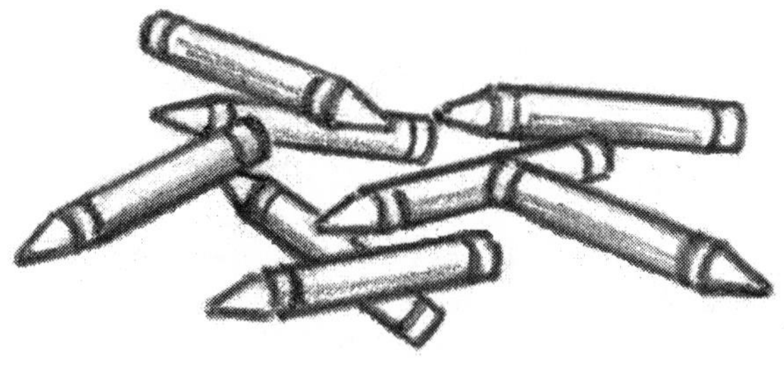

RetroClipArt.com

To everyone, I say let's take whatever time and as much searching in our thinking as necessary to get where we really need to be. Like Abraham Lincoln said, *"my legs are long enough to reach the ground."*

Besides, writing a book is easy when you just write what you are thinking. You don't need to do much research and the number of citations is minimal.

6

CHANGE OF DIRECTION

RetroClipArt.com

The late Yogi Berra once said *"when you come to a fork in the road, take it."* I know some folks who insist on taking the wrong direction every time. I do that sometimes, myself.

Sometimes each of us may need to take a different approach in life. A change in perspective is often necessary for finding the best direction.

This reminds me of Aunt Minnie Pearl, of Grand Ole Opry Fame, talking about her brother. Seems Brother (that's what she called him) had a mule with very long ears and the mule would not enter the barn since the barn door was too short. A friend of Brother suggested that he dig out some extra space from the ground below the door for the mule. Brother replied that the mule's legs are not the problem; it is the mule's ears that won't go into the barn. Seems there's a lot of education that can be learned from knowing about mules, "hear-tell" Brother and my grandfather.

Then there's the story about a boy named Johnny who was late for school one day. Teacher asked *"Johnny why are you late for school?"* Johnny replied *"mam you know it rained last night so much that the steep hill between here and the house was so slick that every time I took one step up that hill, I sled backwards two steps."* Teacher says *"my goodness, Johnny how in the world did you finally get here?"* Johnny, *"mam I just turned around and headed back home and the first thing I knew I was right here at school."* Seems some of us could use a little change in our direction in order to get somewhere. On occasion, my wife provides me with that advice.

Since this book merely contains my thoughts as they unfold, I will not attempt to abide by all the correct writing rules.[29] I may repeat myself a few times as it becomes fitting to the thoughts at hand.

Once, I attempted to correct the grammar of Papa Jim. He immediately (you understand how quick that was and what it meant

---

[29] If you paid full-price for your copy you are free to make your own corrections.

in the nineteen-fifties[30] when used by a grandfather don't you?) informed me that *"I understood what he said!"* You know something, he was correct. I always understood what he meant clearly. The corrections I offered him were not necessary at all.

And he really didn't like to repeat himself, either. On occasion, due to my lapses in memory, Papa Jim did remind me of the fact that he disliked needing to repeat his words to me. He was big on learning retention.

I may repeat a few things in this book, either, due to my weakness in memory or the need for both of us (readers and author) to be reunited with substantive matters of relevance and understanding.

Anyway, you can take a crayon to your copy of this book and fix it up anyway you see fit. I assume that you did pay full price for your copy. (If you didn't, just send the balance directly to me and I will take your name off of the usual suspects list.) Besides, you can't change my thoughts anyway, just your own. I'm at least as stubborn as you are.

I will stick to my thoughts and not put anything extra in. You can identify the blanks and fill them in yourself. Anyway, I can't seem to think of a single thing I forgot. It is okay if you sometimes pause to do some of your own thinking too. I use a lot of commas, short paragraphs, and etc. to let you insert your thoughts. If you do your part, you should be pleased with this book when you have finished it. You can change whatever you wish, especially your thinking. That is, if you have remitted full-price for your copy. You do have your own copy, don't you? Remember that God is watching us and He may take the crayon away from both of us.

I don't know whether this is a short or long book, but I will quit writing when I can't think of anything else within five minutes. If you

---

[30] You are getting old when you have to identify the millennium.

have more thoughts of your own, you can continue on as long as you like. Just have your crayons handy. If I come up with something later I will just start a new book. Since I don't procrastinate much on things that I can do entirely without, then we should get to the end of this commotion in reasonable time.

Then sometimes later does not always get here right away. I didn't even get my birthmark until I was five years old. Papa Jim put it there for me.[31] Who knows when this thing will come to an end, unless you go ahead and take a peek at the end right now? That's an opportunity that you have now (yours) that I don't have yet (mine).

O' yes, I think and communicate in first person, don't you? I never have understood why a writer should refer to himself (or herself) as if they were somebody else. This reminds me of just being "beside" myself. Or is it "ahead" of myself? It is more likely for me to be "behind" myself.

Reminds me of actors who pretend to be someone else. The actors take on the persona of the person they portray to their fans. (Why do we have to do this?) Of course, the actor is herself/himself. Who would you expect them to be? Just maybe, they might choose to pretend to be someone else. But when you observe their personal life you often see someone who is very different from the roles they play as actors.[32] Many people pretend to be someone else depending on who they are in the presence of.

---

[31] This was another impressionable moment in my life that might be considered illegal today. I see this birthmark as a reminder of what's really in my best interest during life.

[32] I recently watched the Oscars presentation on TV. It was difficult for me to connect some of these people to the characters they played in the movies I saw. The film editor must have left large portions of filming on the cutting room floor. You would think that the messages in some of these movies would affect the actor's lives in better ways.

(Most of us behaved differently in the presence of our mother and grandmothers. Did you?)

Now, let us return to the sentence we are in. (Don't you just love these little "side bars" in the middle of the main event. I learned that one from a high profile televised court case. They don't make the best ones up. The real ones are better.)

Another friend of mine, Curtis Easter, is allegedly noted as having come in third in a Curtis Easter "look-alike" contest. A couple of other people beat him out. Curtis did brag to the second-place finisher that he came in next to last while Curtis came in third. (There were only three finishers in the contest, as the rest of the contestants looked more like themselves.) That's vintage Curtis. Curtis just hangs around, to some extent, in spite of himself. Hear tell, though, he was relieved by the outcome of the contest. He was momentarily afraid that he might be mistaken for himself. Curtis, like most of us, would like to get away from ourselves occasionally. For the most part, I have been stuck with myself just about the whole time. Someday I hope to get away from myself for a little while. My wife thinks that would be nice, too. Then on the other hand, that other fella looks a little scary. Maybe the devil I know is better than the one I don't know.

On one occasion I did get one up on Curtis. He was pushing me around somewhat on the status of "who's who" among us. I told Curtis that I could hold one position that he could never qualify for: *"I could be his assistant; that he could never be."*

One more first thing (not sure what the limit is on first things): I never really understood why the first part of a book should be called the "Foreword." Is it like the golf term, "fore," used to warn someone to "watch out" because something that can strike you is on the way moving in your direction? Is there a middle word? Is the middle word followed by the afterword? The thought of a last word really scares me. It sounds fatal to me. Reminds me of the fella who came running right through the reception area straight to the doctor hollering, *"Quick Doc, do something for me! My lifetime guaranteed fountain pen just quit!"* What is a last first word? Who really cares? Should you use more or less words? Why be concerned? Words are plentiful, so use 'em freely. They are everywhere.

7

ON WITH IT

RetroClipArt.com

"Hop to it!"

Enough said with these first things and warnings. I need to get on with this book before JR gives up on me. He wants to hear what God has to say. However, I need to head to a Holiday Inn Express now to spend the night so that I can qualify as an author.[33] Many

[33] Holiday Inn Express advertised their services at one time with a TV ad in which an otherwise unqualified person would infer themselves as being an expert in some immediately needed skill situation simply because they had spent the night in a Holiday Inn Express motel.

people obtain their expert status qualifications by spending a night in a Holiday Inn Express. Others just claim their credibility through a mail order certificate purchase. For some credibility gaps there is a gullibility fill.

Some are just smarter than others. Take the kid who enters a barber shop and the barber whispers to his customer, *"This is the dumbest kid in the world. Watch while I prove it to you."*

> The barber puts a dollar bill in one hand and two quarters in the other, then calls the kid over and asks, *"Which do you want, son?"*
>
> The kid takes the quarters and leaves.
>
> *"What did I tell you?"* said the barber. *"That kid never learns!"*
>
> Later, when the customer leaves, he sees the kid coming out of the ice cream store.
>
> *"Hey! May I ask you a question? Why did you take the quarters instead of the dollar bill?"*
>
> The kid licked his cone and replied, *"Because the day I take the dollar, the game is over."*

That kid was not so dumb, after all. Maybe, the people calling others *"dummy"* are the real "dummies."

Then some of us are just plain "hardheaded." I was in a business meeting one time with two business partners who were going at it, each with some sense of fortification. (Curtis had hair on his head and Bill did not.) Eventually, Curtis tells Bill that *"his head is so hard that hair cannot grow in it."* (Needless to say, the meeting ended suddenly.)

O yes, I was about to forget the most important "fore warning." I really meant for this version of the book to be for us fellas as women think and communicate differently than us guys. I really don't feel qualified to write for women. We fellas need our little ole "powder room" too. I was hoping one of you ladies might translate this book into "women talk" and get me out of trouble. Don't really want to upset you ladies. It's sort of like the message of the words "woman" on the door that seems to say to us guys that this is the forbidden room. Reminds me, again, that my grandfather had a male mule and he used to say *"whoa mule"* when he wanted that mule to stop right where he is. No offense meant ladies, just a fence to keep me from harm. I will "whoa" on this subject right here.

Yes, ladies, I know a man's perspective is misguided as soon as we men begin to think. Reminds me, again, of "Hagar the Horrible" explaining to the doctor that he cannot see his toes when he looks down. Hagar wants to know whether or not he has an eye problem. The doctor replies, *"No, you have a size problem."* Hagar responds, *"So, you're saying my toes are too small?"*[34]

Oops, my wife just said it would be okay for you ladies to read this book if you have your own copy and it is fully paid for at the regular price. She is already correcting me. She said that you other ladies would be able to straighten this whole thing out along with your husbands. Hum, how do the ladies do this? I haven't even gotten into the main text and my wife is already setting me straight. Where do they get their information?

C. S. Lewis once (or more times) made smiles with this line: *"Husbands were made to be talked to. It helps them concentrate their*

---

[34] "Hagar The Horrible" in *The State Newspaper*, p. C6, April 28, 2015.

minds on what they're reading." Or in my case, writing. Remember that I tried to keep this book just among us guys. But if your sweetie continues, just remember to nod your head in her direction occasionally in order to keep her on her track instead of yours.

I remember that a friend of my wife phoned one day when my wife was out (that is, out of sight). The caller was content to tell me that the call was not important; she just wanted to talk. So I told her that I would lay the phone on the kitchen table and she could talk as long as she wished. I guess she finished talking quickly because the phone went to the dial tone immediately. O well, it is getting very difficult to please some people.

Enough said about things and warnings. (JR is getting edgy!) My thoughts are turning to what goes in this book now. So on with the book. Get your crayons ready so you can add your part.

8

THE STARTING WORDS

(Preamble)

RetroClipArt.com

"Start here!"

Webster seems to think that the word "preamble" is a noun fittingly expressing the purpose of something that follows. Possibly this is a good place to establish a measured foundation for the substance of this book. I like to think of it as a memorandum of understanding of what is about to take place. Call it a "preamble" if you wish.

It is an awesome and courageous undertaking when one represents an interview with God. First, one must acknowledge their belief in God which is faith-based. Then one must recognize a legitimate source of God's Words. Historical evidence points to the Bible as the means through which God speaks to us today. And, of course, God's power and divine nature have been clearly seen and understood from what has been made (created), so that mankind is without excuse. {Romans 1:20}

There is no common foundation for a debate between a believer and a non-believer. The believer has faith; the non-believer has none, so there is no common realm for their exchange. There is no logical ground for debate, it's not dialectic. It's like one is talking about a football game while the other is talking about opera, the language for each is very different. My wife sometimes illustrates this by saying *"do you take your lunch to work or do you ride the bus?"* In this book, the God of reference is viewed as the one and only Supreme, Creator God who has all power over everything. He is the alpha and omega. He is the center point in a concentric circle. He, also, connects the circle at the apex. (Ponder that one again if you will, as we discussed it previously.) The non-believer does not share such a faith-based common foundation basis for discussion. The Bible is seen by non-believers as being synthetic.

The non-believer sees creation as a scientific-happening while the believer views the scientific evidence as merely a discovery of the process by which the Creator caused the whole thing to happen.

According to Hebrews 11:3, our faith is necessary to understand that the universe was formed of God's command. This means that what is seen was not made of what was visible. Yet, God provides us with mental evidence as a further foundation for the development of our faith. I like to refer to it as *"faith under construction."* Since the invisible cannot be observed with the human eye we must depend on symbolism for our mental images in order to bring an abstraction to our comprehension. God gave us the perfect means for doing this. It is called *"mathematics"* and we use it every day. It is the common language describing matter and motion as it comes from God using only one dialect for its vocabulary.

RetroClipArt.com

The following comments were developed during several years of study by the author. The source of what follows comes as a synthesis from reading many books on mathematics, logic, and religion; listening to what others have to say, tiresome searches through the worldwide internet, much contemplation, my own logical thinking, and serious intensive prayer. I not only had to "think outside the box," I had to step completely out of the box many times.

I would love to cite all the great thoughts that I have observed from others and benefited from, but there are so many disconnected fragments that the references would be too extensive. Too, many of my comments in this book are constructed from many fragments taken out of the context intended by the authors. Most of the authors I have read were studying mathematics for the sake of science and their own theorems. Some authors looked to the Bible to explain mathematics. I looked to mathematics to reveal God. Some looked to mathematics to discover and express forms, shapes, and movements. I looked to mathematics to discover and describe the fundamentals of God's creative genius. By my propositions offered in this book, I would be guilty of improperly misrepresenting the sources I observed. They mostly stimulated my thinking otherwise. I did not fabricate. I looked to discover how God transfigured all creation to His Glory. So, let's go onward with the results.

As noted earlier, a concentric circle is used symbolically to represent God in this book. Mathematics is seen to be a neutral subject by some. Neutral means indifferent or "not engaged on either side. It is not aligned with a political or ideological grouping. Many regard mathematics as a subject that is "not engaged" and "not aligned" with either Biblical or worldly thinking. Some learned persons believe that mathematics is independent from God. They would approach mathematics as a "safe" subject. A safe subject is one we can all see the same way, regardless of any of our beliefs. For example, the equation one plus one equals two ("1 + 1 = 2") works the same way for an atheist, Muslim, Hindu, Buddhist, or Christian. Mathematics is seen by many as a subject of numbers and facts void of any bias; as opposed to the supposition of something or a belief about something.

But is mathematics really indifferent and neutral? Is such a thing even possible? The Bible warns us that we are in a spiritual warfare. {Ephesians 6:10-18} The Bible urges us to guard our heart and to test the spirit behind what we are taught. {First John 4:1; Proverbs 4:23} The Bible does not mention any neutral ground. According to the

Bible, nothing can really be neutral. Everything will be presented in either a biblical or a worldly fashion.

So how can mathematics be viewed biblically? What does God have to do with mathematics? Is there an insight into mathematics that helps us see God in absolute terms of logic that appear as factual reality without bias?

We begin by looking at an equation we are all familiar with: "1 + 1 = 2." We will examine where this equation came from and why it works. As we examine this equation's origins and ability to work, we will discover some startling truths applicable to every area of mathematics revealing God's all-encompassing creation of everything except sin.

Throughout history, mathematicians have developed various theories to explain the origin and consistency of addition. Some doubters have speculated that addition exists by sheer chance. Of course, others have claimed man created addition and addition works because man designed it to work.

I have never found a mathematics textbook that even attempts to offer an explanation for "addition's" existence. Throughout my schooling, not one of my textbooks ever explained where addition originated or why it works. I eventually came to the realization that addition, along with all other mathematical facts, is an evolved, self-existent truth. This position fits well with Plato and Aristotle's definition of truth. They say that the opinions we hold are true when they assert that which is, really is, or that which is not, really is not. When the "is" of a statement agrees with the way things are, the statement is true.

While all this exercise in deductive thinking that follows does help us along the way, it does not supersede God's explanations. The Bible gives us a radically different explanation for addition.

While the Bible does not specifically say, *"This is where addition came from and why it works,"* the Bible offers us principles that apply to addition, as well as to every other aspect of mathematics. Look at what just two Bible verses reveal.

The verse *"For by him all things were created"* {Colossians 1:16} tells us where addition originated. It tells us God created "all" things. The word "all" includes everything, even mathematics. This does not mean God created the symbols 1 and 2. Man developed those symbols using the mind that God created in mankind in the same way as God allowed Adam to name the living creatures. {Genesis 2:19} Some of these symbols represent a real-life principle called addition that is embedded in everything around us (a principle God created.) For example, we have often taken an object, added another object or more to it, and found ourselves with a new third object (such as when we take some flour and add some milk; smash it around and apply some heat we come up with some bread). It does not matter what we attempt to add, objects add predictably. Our whole money exchange system works the same. We all add money as we engage in economic transactions. Addition works the same way for everybody. Why? This is true because all things add in a regular, precise manner (axiomatically.) We refer to this regularity as the "addition principle."

God created this principle that prevails throughout everything at all times. When God created all things, He determined how they would operate. He chose to make different aspects of creation to operate according to the same reliable principle we call "addition." Man developed different symbols and systems, using the mental facilities that God created in man, to describe or represent the observed orderly way in which everything works while discovering God's laws of relationships and movements. God determined the way in which the things mathematics represents behave. Symbols become necessary for mankind to recognize and express how things happen and relate. The reality that mathematics represents originated with God.

Now that we know where addition originated, let us look at why addition works. We will find the answer in another verse in Colossians, which reads, *"In him all things hold together."* {Colossians 1:17} Since the word "all" includes addition, God not only created addition but also continually holds the entire universe together with addition and other principles of mathematics. The sun, the moon, earth, and all the other planets and objects in space seem to hold their places steadily. All the service systems of planet earth appear to function such as gravity, oxygen, water, light, temperature, and food within a relational model that can be described mathematically. For example, the Maxwell equations can be associated with God's statement recorded in Genesis 1:5, "let there be light." The Maxwell equations are the set of four fundamental equations governing electromagnetism (i.e., the behavior of electric and magnetic fields). They were first written down in complete form by physicist James Clerk Maxwell, who added the so-called displacement current term to the final equation, although steady-state forms were known earlier.

Scientists have discovered a lot about the predictable way objects continually combine. This is often mistaken as evolution rather than transformation. Transformation is how God holds everything together dynamically allowing His creativity to extend forward to form new phenomenon. Addition is simply a name for the predictable way objects combine. God holds everything together by keeping objects combining consistently. Otherwise, everything would collapse. Objects do not go from chaos to stability. It is just the opposite. Death and decay is the natural progressive law of God caused by and driven by sin. This process is both an affect and an effect.

Can you imagine what would happen if objects did not consistently combine in the same way? If the equation "1 + 1 = 2" only worked some of the time then it would not be plausible. Mathematics as we know it would be useless! We could not rely on those steady facts and consistent processes to work in the physical world. Mathematics is consistent and reliable because God consistently holds every part and process of the universe in its place. God's faithfulness in holding this universe together ensures us that objects will add in a predictable manner and that the equation "1 + 1 = 2" will consistently work. Mathematics is not independent from God. It is not neutral. Mathematics' very existence and ability to work is dependent on God's faithfulness in holding everything together!

The principles we have discovered about the addition equation "1 + 1 = 2" apply to the rest of mathematics. Like addition, all of mathematics is a way of visualizing and expressing the laws and relationships God created. Mathematics works because God faithfully holds everything in place.

God's faithfulness not only makes mathematics useful to us, but it also communicates an important message. The Bible tells us that God established the "fixed laws" of heaven and earth. In Jeremiah 33:25-26 God said *"If I have not established my covenant with day and night and the fixed laws of heaven and earth, then I will reject the descendants of Jacob and David my servant."*

Mathematics is really a testimony to God's existence. Some mathematicians have postulated that Euler's Identify formula proves the existence of God:

$$e^\wedge(pi * i) + 1 = 0$$

Where

> e is Euler's number, the base of natural logarithms,
> i is the imaginary unit, which satisfies $i^2 = -1$, and
> *pi* is π, the ratio of the circumference of a circle to its diameter.

Euler's Identity formula is named after the Swiss mathematician Leonhard Euler (1707-1783). It is considered an example of "mathematical beauty" because of its feasible symmetry.

Three of the basic arithmetic operations occur exactly once each: addition, multiplication, and exponentiation. The identity also links five fundamental mathematical constants:

- The number 0, the additive identity.
- The number 1, the multiplicative identity.
- The number *PI*, which is ubiquitous in the geometry of Euclidean space and analytical mathematics (*PI* = 3.14159265...)
- The number *e*, the base of natural logarithms, which occurs widely in mathematical analysis ($e = 2.718281828...$).
- The number *i*, the imaginary unit of the complex numbers, a field of numbers that contains the roots of all polynomials (that are not constants), and whose study leads to deeper insights into many areas of algebra and calculus.

(Both *PI* and *e* are transcendental numbers.)

Furthermore, the equation is given in the form of an expression set equal to zero, which is common practice in several areas of mathematics.

Edward Kasner and James Newman in *Mathematics and the Imagination* note, *"We can only reproduce the equation and not stop to inquire into its implications. It appeals equally to the mystic, the scientist, the mathematician."*

This formula unites the five most important symbols of mathematics: 1, 0, *pi*, *e* and *i* (the square root of minus one). This union was regarded as a mystic union containing representatives from each branch of the mathematical tree: arithmetic is represented by 0 and 1, algebra by the symbol *i*, geometry by *pi*, and analysis by the transcendental *e*. Harvard mathematician Benjamin Pierce said about the formula, *"That is surely true, it is absolutely paradoxical; we cannot understand it, and we don't know what it means, but we have proved it, and therefore we know it must be the truth."*

Most students who took their mathematics classes seriously understand the mathematicians' method for mathematical proof. In this case, the proof would proceed as follows.

Suppose that God does not exist:

Then *e*^(*pi* **i*) + 1 does not = 0.

Thus, if *e*^(*pi* **i*) + 1 = 0, God must Exist.

We can only say that Euler's Identity formula is absolutely paradoxical; we cannot understand it fully, and we don't know what it means other than it demonstrates mathematical perfection. We have proved it within the established laws of mathematics, and therefore we know it must be the truth. It does provide representational faithfulness (to that end it works!) Once again, we stand in awe before the supremacy of God in the order of the universe. This examination of mathematics demolishes any idea of randomness or chance in the creation of earth and everything on earth and the heavens.

Euler's Identity equation is the equality represented in this book by the concentric circle, which is used to form a perfect sphere.

There are many who rise up at this moment and charge people like me with the *Texas Sharpshooter Fallacy*. This charge accuses us of starting with our conclusion, and then picking our facts to support our hypothesis.

The fallacy's name comes from a parable in which a Texan fires his gun at the side of a barn, paints a bullseye around the bullet hole, and claims to be a sharpshooter. Though the shot may have been totally random, he makes it appear as though he has performed a highly non-random act. In normal target practice, the bullseye defines a region of significance, and there's a low probability of hitting it by firing in a random direction. However, when the region of significance is determined after the event has occurred, any outcome at all can be made to appear spectacularly improbable.

The *Texas Sharpshooter Fallacy* claims that we Christians use the same data to both construct and test a hypothesis. A hypothesis must be constructed before data is collected based on that hypothesis. If one data set is used to construct a hypothesis, then a new data set must be generated (ideally, in a different way, based on predictions made by the hypothesis) to test it.

I would agree with these critics if I were attempting to do what they claim I am doing. From my viewpoint, mathematics is descriptive by nature rather than creative. Mathematics experiments and describes relationships among numbers, shapes, and quantities. It uses signs, symbols, and proofs and includes arithmetic, algebra, calculus, geometry, and trigonometry. The proofs examine relational validity. Even within this science, not all variables are dependent variables, nor do all independent variables drive a dependent variable.

To me, when you look at the uses of mathematics that follow we are not being deterministic. We are discovering and describing objects as they exist and as they behave. The proponents that follow are not really claiming that any of this mathematics actually defines God or even determines any outcomes. The mathematics used simply puts the pieces into a mosaic that represents much of God's creative architecture. We refer to it as a way of providing digital imagery of how it all fits to together and functions, both fixed structures (algebra, geometry, trigonometry, etc.) and changes (calculus). We are only claiming that it provides evidence (proof) that the universe is the result of an intelligent design by the architect and builder (God.)

The following image is my favorite reminder of identity mathematics. I don't know where it came from or who wrote it. It has circulated around in the public domain for several years. I make no claim of it as mine. The anonymous author captures the essence of God as conveyed in mathematics.

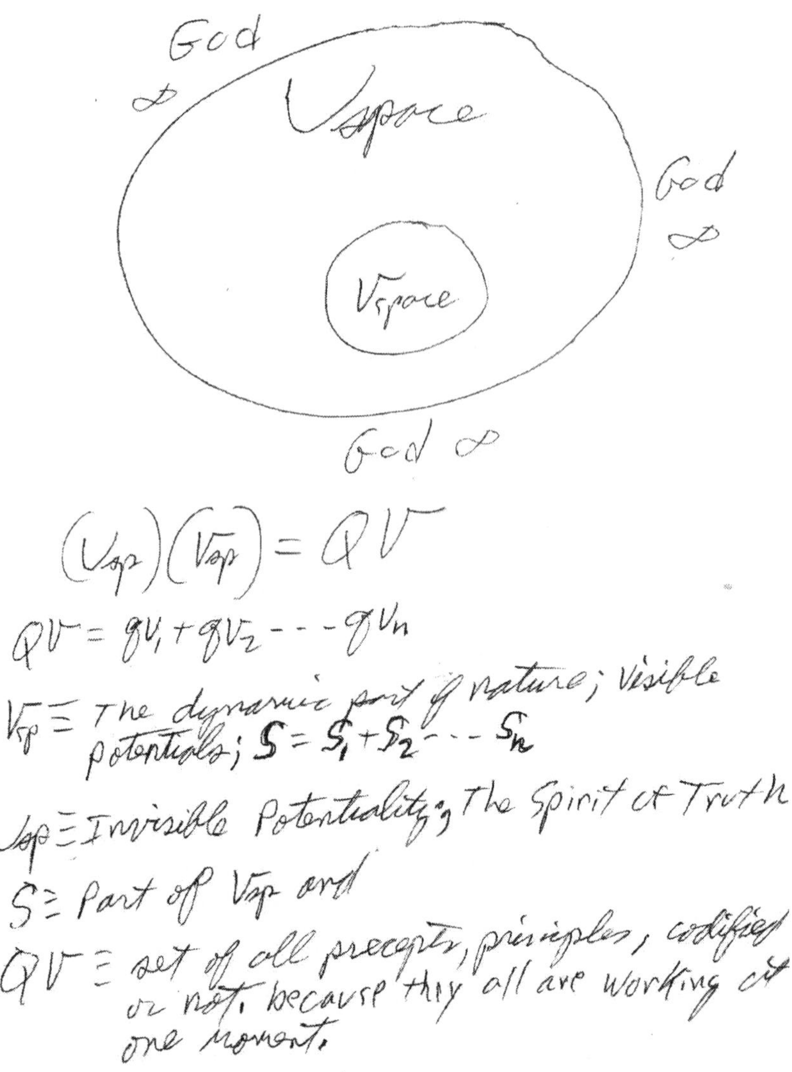

Anonymous

Because these points of view are so important to establishing one's foundation for faith, I must cite another case where mathematics testifies to the existence and power of God, the same as nature does. Both nature and mathematics demonstrate the manifestations of God's splendor in what He has rendered into existence.

Scientists working in the UK have discovered robust evidence that the creation of the earth and moon was a deliberately calculated act. The researchers found that the earth, moon, and beyond were engineered according to a specific equation. They have dubbed it the "God Equation." The equation can be expressed as follows.

$$(HI_f.\pi) \div \Omega = C_o$$

It shows a constant, unchanging relationship between the speed of light, the ratio between the circumference and diameter of a circle, and the radio frequency of hydrogen in space. Artificial intelligence engineer David Cumming, CEO of the Edinburgh-based company Intelligent Earth, recently discovered the equation, and said: *"I am a scientist and as such I didn't at first really believe it myself. But physics is physics, and maths[sic] is maths[sic], and you can't argue with it."*

The discovery of the equation began with research by engineer Professor Alexander Thom (1894-1985) of Oxford University, into the properties of megalithic constructions such as Stonehenge. He found that their construction did not follow existing measurement systems, but it did fit into a pattern of specific lengths which he called megalithic yards. Two independent researchers, Christopher Knight and Alan Butler, based in York, then, showed that the megalithic system of measurement was directly derived from characteristics of the Earth's movements through space.

Linking this system of measurements with known constants such as *PI* (π, the relationship between the circumference and diameter of a circle), HI_f (the radio frequency of the hydrogen fine transition in space,) Ω (0.0123456789 representing all the characters of the base 10 number system), and the speed of light in a vacuum C_o (which = 299,792.458 km/sec), and building on research by

Knight and Butler, and the work of Professor Alexander Thom, former Reading University doctoral researcher; Cumming followed a research program that resulted in his discovery of what is called the "God Equation." Researchers were startled when they observed that the God Equation shows a direct link between the speed of light, the radio frequency of hydrogen in space, *pi*, and earth's orbit, rotation and weight. As the possibility of the Earth having the exact required characteristics to fit the equation by chance is remote, and the equation has, in theory, been in existence since the beginning of the Universe. This means that the Earth's orbit, rotation, and weight must have been engineered to fit this equation or we can say that the equation describes the attributes of Earth. I prefer the later as it avoids the *Texas Trigger Fallacy* tag.

Glory belongs to God the designer and creator! Through the lenses of mathematics, I can see the shadows of the abstract work of God and proof it using God's "Laws of Mathematics."

To the best of my many years of searching, I cannot find anything that cannot be represented using mathematics. Recently, the use of cellulose material coated with an emulsion sensitive to light (film) has been displaced with digital photography and digital video media. Now the "global warming" advocates make their claims using mathematics. Politicians appear to pay a lot of attention to the numbers in public opinion polls. Forecasting would be a mere "happen-stance" without the predictability of observed relationships and trends. And what would you do with a bank draft that contained no money amount!

Of course, we cannot leave Albert Einstein out of this discussion. His Theory of Relativity is monumental and demonstrates, again, the intelligent design of the universe. In 1915, he devised the Einstein field equations which relate the curvature of space-time with the mass, energy, and momentum within it.

$$E = mc^2$$

"Do you doubt this one?"

General relativity is a theory of gravitation whose defining feature is its use of the Einstein field equations. The solutions of the field equations are metric tensors which define the topology of the space-time and how objects react inertially[35] to the presence or absence of directional forces. The theory of relativity is used in many of our modern electronics such as the Global Positioning System (GPS). GPS systems work with excellent precision because of the Theory of Relativity.

I like to think that GPS stands for "God's Perfect System." The Global Positioning System certainly demonstrates God's perfection through mathematics.

"Unbelievers" just don't get it. They are missing the necessary ingredient: faith. We "believers" see it plainly as we allow God to show it to us. We just don't attempt to get there on our own.

Too, all of this intellectual activity shows us our ability to think, reason, and understand in combination with knowledge. Maybe, this is where we begin to understand what we are. Mankind has been created in the very likeness of God. Surely this cannot mean that the likeness is a physical resemblance, since God existed before anything physical came into being. Therefore, it probably suggests that, like God, human beings are essentially spiritual beings. While

---

[35] The property of a body by which it remains at rest or continues moving in a straight line unless acted upon by a directional force.

on earth we are wrapped in a physical body having intelligence, moral consciousness, and freedom of choice.

It is when creation takes place and physical objects come into existence that the language of mathematics begins to communicate to the very soul of man. Mathematics, like language, serves to communicate to the mind of man's soul. Do you hear God speaking? He sometimes speaks through mathematics the same as He does through nature and the Bible.

The greatest application of mathematics by God may be seen in the structure of a human being. The very hairs on our head are all numbered. {Matthew 10:30} The sheer genius of God is displayed dynamically as we view the anatomy of the human body and its coordinated functioning. Yet we witness infinite uniqueness as seen in the DNA metrics and the patterns of finger prints. Even the study of behavioral science by mankind is seen as a set of very complex mathematical patterns.

Failures of mankind can be demonstrated as errors in applying mathematical relationships the same as when we misunderstand what anyone has said to us. The Gateway Arch in Saint Louis, MO was planned properly, but the construction of the arch by man was off at the apex. Some stress exists caused by forcing the two segments of the arch together at the top when they did not exactly meet together, as previously calculated mathematically.

The worst misapplication of God's design is demonstrated in sin. God did not build sin. Man did that one all by himself with the help of Satan.

Faith does not happen without a firm foundation for comprehending what you believe. I leave the atheist to continue to discover God's Laws of Mathematics and the extensive use to which God created. Maybe, this could be the explanation of what

God meant when He said that He spoke everything into existence. He may have been speaking metaphorically. We cannot escape the realms of a concentric circle. It is a perfect sphere filled with mathematics all relating everything to God Himself. We are located in the area somewhere.

The "unbelievers," should think of abandoning their procrastination and examine the topology of creation. "Topology" is the study of the properties of geometric figures that are independent of size or shape and are not changed by stretching, bending, or twisting. Therein may be discovered the very depth of the meaning of "eternity."

As to procrastination, I have resolved to quit putting off things that I am never going to do anyway. I have simply quit procrastinating all together, and focused on the things that I must do that are critical to me now and hereafter.

Follow-up: It you desire further study or wish to reference some of the above discussions, I suggest that we be practical. You can surf the internet and find tons of information about all the points I have made above. If I were to provide a reference list here, it could become longer than this entire book as it exists presently. I cannot fathom how many hits you could get by typing in "Albert Einstein." You may want to enter "Euler," "David Cumming," "The God Formula" or "The Equation of Creation." You will find plenty of information relating to these comments. Some of it is intellectual, while some of it is bias to a pre-conceived point of view. If you have a problem with any of this, you should ask God to guide you. It is called prayer, and God has the "Final Word." So consult with Him.

9

ARE YOU EXPECTING ANYONE TO BELIEVE THIS?

RetroClipArt.com

Another friend of mine, Thomas is a bit skeptical. He is probably asking about now: *"Jim, really, did you have an interview with God?"* Umm, kind of so, just follow me further. I did ask the questions.

Hum, err, the answers? Well, you just read this book and decide for yourself. God has been known to speak through a whole host of means: angels, dreams, burning bushes, whirlwinds and particular the Bible. He speaks to us mostly in the form of revelation. Actually the book of Genesis is also a book of revelation as God reveals the startup of the whole "shebang." That is the earth and mankind.

There, you evolutionists. Yes, I said *"shebang."* Actually you folks are pretty good at discovering the processes God used in creation. However, you seem to skip God, though, when you don't have a provable linkage or you run out of origins. (I'll have to say about this point later.) To say it evolved without a designer/maker is the same as saying *"it just happened."* When you leave God out at this point you are leaving a very deep dark-hole in your explanation. What say you then? Nothing results in nothing when you have nothing to start with.

My friend, Thomas (he is of the doubting kind) said to me, *"O come on Jim, God is just in your imagination."* Now right here is where I want to preface this entire exposition. The discovery of God begins within your mind which is the seat of consciousness, in which thinking, feelings, etc. takes place. The mind is the portal to your soul. Virtually it is your soul as it is the sole image of your consciousness which is life itself. It's that simple.

God entrusted to us a mind with boundless ability, the ability to possess knowledge, formulate opinions, make decisions, and direct action. At some point we will be held accountable for our use of the mind. It is good, therefore to make the following observations.

The foundation of genuine religion is faith. By its very nature faith must be based on something other than absolute proof. Once one establishes proof through personal direct examination he no longer has need for faith. In accordance with this principle the

Bible teaches that faith comes by hearing testimony, not by seeing absolute reality. You can practice faith with your eyes closed.

Belief can be a dangerous trap since human nature is slow to accept that which deviates from one's established pattern of thought. Some accept everything that their parents, tutors, and associates believe. They defend these positions as they might defend property rights they have gained through inheritance. Others accept only what they desire, even at the expense of personal integrity. Demosthenes admirably assessed the matter when he said, *"nothing is so easy to deceive as one's self; for what we wish, that we readily believe."*

Truth is the only valid principle upon which we can establish a sound belief. However, it is easy to bargain away this principle for something else. Oddly enough, man is the only creature who attempts to bargain. A dog, for example, will not exchange his bone with another dog no matter the size of the other bone. (The dog will likely want both bones without negotiation.) Man will exchange truth for something of less value and not even realize his loss.

As stated earlier, Plato and Aristotle define truth. They say that the opinions we hold are true when they assert that which is, really is, or that which is not, really is not. When the "is" of a statement agrees with the way things are, the statement is true. It is easy to understand this definition but difficult to apply it in any given instance. Finally, pursuit of truth, according to this definition, once it is found, is most difficult of all.

Truth must never be confused with personal judgment. When one says, for example, *"Gentlemen prefer blondes,"* there is nothing in the nature of gentlemen or blondes which makes it necessary for men to always prefer blondes. This is a matter of personal judgment and not a universal truth. On the other hand when one says, *"The whole is always greater than any of its parts,"* this is an absolute fact. It is a unique quality of man to be able to reason this way and to know the difference in fact and judgment. That is when he proceeds without prejudice.

It is this ability to reason which leads us to believe that everything must have a creator, including the seeds of life forms. It is reasonable to recognize that matter is contingent on something greater than matter itself. Observe any living thing, with or without a soul, as it passes through the gates of death; since it cannot save itself, it must not be the originator of itself.

When asked by a lawyer to identify the most important rule in life, Jesus replied, *"You shall love the Lord your God with all your HEART, with all your SOUL, with your entire MIND, and with all your STRENGTH."* {Mark 12:30} It is interesting to note that Jesus added the word *"mind"* to this command which was introduced in Deuteronomy 6:5 without the word *"mind."* This would seem to emphasize the need to understand what God has to say while we have a fleshly brain. When Jesus added the word *"mind"* He was saying *"you shall love God with everything you have and everything you are while you are human, using all the available strength you have within your consciousness."* That is you must intentionally love God with understanding of what you are doing.[36]

I know another doubter,[37] other than Thomas, who claims to be

---

[36] Dictionaries typically define *heart* as "the vital center of one's being, emotions, and sensibilities." *Soul* is typically defined as "the animating and vital principle in man, credited with the faculties of thought, action, and emotion and often conceived as an immaterial entity." *Mind* is typically defined as "the human consciousness that originates in the brain and is manifested in thought, perception, feeling, will, memory, or imagination which is the intellectual or rational faculty in man."

[37] I will not mention his name, but I will pray for him.

an atheist. Occasionally he challenges my belief in God. He says that I am too smart to believe in an invisible deity. I just keep posing to him a risk/reward based outcome problem to solve. Simply, if he is correct I do not really face any long-term negative consequences. His position does not hold a promise of punishment in the hereafter for me. However, if I am correct he faces an extremely negative outcome that will last for a very long-time into eternity, himself. My position promises him severe pain and sorrow in the hereafter. My position promises me joy, peace, and happiness. I cannot lose with my position either way.

Is it possible to imagine a time when nothing existed? Take away everything and then you have to begin somewhere, because here we are today. Surely it must have had a beginning. The entire universe exists. Where did it come from? How did it begin? Why am I here? For what purpose, if any, did it happen?

Some say it all happened by chance, without any reason or purpose whatever. But given what appears to be intelligent design and order throughout the universe (we can observe), an origin by chance seems hard to accept. And life without meaning, seems clearly contrary to the very mind (that I have) which searches for meaning.

10

A FIRST CAUSE

RetroClipArt.com

"God said so!"

Man sees only what has been created: the natural world. The simple statement that God created the heavens and the earth is one of the most challenging concepts confronting the modern mind. We hear from the scholarly community that the vast galaxy we live in is spinning at the incredible speed of 400,000 miles an hour. But even at this breakneck speed, our galaxy still needs 200 million years to make one rotation. In addition to our own galaxy there are over one billion other galaxies just like ours in the universe.

Some scientists say that the number of stars in our universe is equal to all the grains of sands on all the beaches on earth. Yet this complex sea of spinning stars functions with remarkable order and efficiency. To say that the universe *"just happened"* or *"evolved"* requires more unquestioning faith in metaphysics than to believe that God is behind these amazing statistics. At least, God's explanation in the Book of Genesis is not fragmented. He presents an explanation that shows a symmetrical mosaic that has no loose ends.

Many will agree that the most basic, fundamental question concerning existence is not that *nothing* is here, but rather that *something* is here. We are a part of some kind of *reality*. We possess a consciousness, an awareness that something is happening that is transpiring, unfolding, taking place, etc. And we are a part of it. The reality borne out of our personal observation and experience is that we reside in a space-time universe (cosmos) which is characterized by a *series of events* in which we are participants. We can see it. It is only natural that we would ask the questions, *"What is it?" "Where did it come from?"* Did the cosmos simply come into being from nothing, or has this material universe of which we are a part always been here? Or did someone or something which transcends the totality of this material universe bring it all into existence and us with it?

These questions relate to the philosophical concept of metaphysics, which is "That division of philosophy which includes ontology, or the science of being and cosmology, or the science of fundamental causes and processes in things."[38] At this fundamental level of inquiry we are left with few possible answers to account for or explain this universe where we reside. The three conventional considerations are:

(1) Something came from nothing. Since nothing cannot produce something by rules of logic (observation, causality), something else must be eternal and necessary. Since any series of events is not eternal (a contradiction), there must be an eternal, necessary something not identical to the space-time universe. This answer defies rationality.

(2) Matter is eternal and capable of producing the existing reality through blind chance. This view is based on *Materialism* (or Naturalism) and *Pantheism*. Both hold the premise that nothing exists beyond matter. Materialism therefore is atheistic by definition. Pantheism is similar but insists that since God does not exist, nature is imbued with "god" in all its parts. That is the doctrine that all forces, manifestations, etc. are God. This means the same as polytheism.

(3) God created the universe. This view, *Theism*, holds forth the assertion that someone both transcends, and did create the material universe of which we are a part.

When man sees the contingent nature of the universe, his reason compels him to postulate a first cause. If the material world originated by chance, by spontaneous generation, or were self-induced, this would imply a miracle greater than man can

---

[38] *Webster's New Collegiate Dictionary* (Springfield, Mass.: G. & C. Merriam Co., Publishers, 1953, s.v. "metaphysics," 528.

understand or believe. Webster defines *"miracle"* as *"an event or action that apparently contradicts known scientific laws."*

"Nothing" cannot suddenly become "something" all by itself. There is no science here at all. Where is the evolution? (Besides we still have the monkey, don't we? The monkey never evolved.) Therefore, a first cause of the universe, greater than the universe itself or any of the parts within it, must be postulated. Since we are part of this system and cannot be as great as the whole, we are unable to rationally comprehend the whole. Beyond the point of understanding our part of the total system, reason fails since we have no criterion upon which to operate. The Creator has therefore given us revelation through which we can see beyond the unseen. Divine testimony, thus, becomes the only source of direction in the world of metaphysics. Only God can reveal the supernatural. We as humans existing on earth can only see that which is natural within that which we can see. That is within the realm of our universe as viewed on and from earth.

To summarize, reason takes us to the point that God is just around the corner where all at once we see God creating the world in a majestic display of power and purpose, culminating with a man and woman made like Him. {Genesis 1: 26, 27} Look around, look in the mirror for the evidence yourself.

Creation is one of the ways God uses to tell us about Himself: *"The heavens declare the glory of God; and the firmament shows His handiwork,"* wrote David. *"Day unto day utters speech, and night unto night reveals knowledge."* {Psalm 19:1-2}

Asaph said. *"Let the heavens declare His righteousness, for God Himself is Judge."* {Psalm 50:6}

Paul wrote, *"For since the creation of the world His invisible attributes are clearly seen, being understood by the things that are made, even His eternal power and Godhead, so that they are without excuse."* {Romans 1:120}

God so loves us and wants us to know Him that He put evidence of Himself everywhere we look. The cosmological argument (first cause) and the teleological argument (argument from design) are two of the many cases for the existence of God, David, however, did not write Psalm 19 (reflected in the cover of this book) to prove God's existence. Rather, already captivated and awed by the immensity and beauty of the skies, he simply declares that God exists. David reflects on how God has revealed Himself to mankind so that we can know Him. As seen in verses 1-6 God reveals Himself through His created works and then in verses 7-14 God reveals Himself through His spoken Word.[39]

This leads us to the question: *"Where did God come from?"* While it is reasonable to ask this question concerning the origin of the universe, it is irrational and nonsensical to ask that same question of God, since it implies to Him characteristics found only in the finite universe where there is space and time. However, something eternal logically must exist outside this space/time continuum. The very question posed reveals the inquirer's fallacy of reasoning from within their space/time context. Logically, something eternal must exist outside both time and space. God has no beginning. HE IS! {Exodus 3:14}

[39] "Consider the Lilies," Julie Ackerman Link, *Our Daily Bread*, February 27, 2014.

11

SOUND FOUNDATION FOR FAITH

RetroClipArt.com

"God put this cornerstone in place!"

The Bible says that *"he who comes to God must believe that He is."* {Hebrews 11:6} In other words, there is a "faith" factor relative to a belief in God's existence. Christians affirm God's existence on the basis of faith, but it is a reasonable faith based on the true nature of the cosmos, not a blind faith. Actually, it takes even more faith for the atheist to believe in his position because he holds to his faith against overwhelming evidence to the contrary without an explanation of initial origins.

An agnostic holds a position which states that *"neither the existence nor the nature of God, nor the ultimate origin of the universe is known or knowable."* [40] When the agnostic says, *"I don't know,"* what is really implied is *"I can't know, you can't know, and nobody else can know, either."*

Let's make it a bit simpler. There tends to be three conscious non-believers.

The <u>first</u> is "dogmatic." Here is a person who already has his mind made up. This person says, *"I don't know, you don't know, and no one can know."* These are the same problems as the atheist above. He must know everything in order to hold this position honestly.

The <u>second</u> is "indifferent." *"I don't know and I don't care."* Someone has noted that this person is both ignorant and apathetic. It is not likely that God would reveal Himself to someone who does not care to know: *"He, who has ears, let him hear."* {Luke 14:35}

The <u>third</u> is "dissatisfied." *"I don't know, but I would like to know."* Hear ye, hear ye! Here is a person who demonstrates openness to truth and a willingness to change his position should he have sufficient reasons that make sense to him. Hopefully, this person is in a temporary path in search of truth which gives way to a more reasonable and less skeptical view of life and the venue of truth.

It is my opinion that when this person seeks God then God will find him and stand by him as long as he listens and obeys God. {Psalms 9:10} This requires that man trust God at all times and prove his trust with his actions of obedience.

---

[40] Webster's New Collegiate Dictionary, s.v. "agnosticism."

Salvation by faith in Christ sounds too easy for many people. They would rather think that they may have done something to save themselves. Their religion becomes one of self-effort that leads either to disappointment or pride, but does not result in salvation.

It is important to understand that man earns nothing by his deeds. Deeds are actions that simply reveal and demonstrate the trust that man places in God. By grace man is saved through his faith, which is a gift of God. {Ephesians 2: 8, 9} Works are simply the evidence of man's faith and the fulfillment of obedience. Good works should be done because we are saved, rather than to be saved. Obedience is an exercise of trust. The conditions of trust that require actions by man relate to the actions of obedience such as:

(1) Hearing and Learning in order to believe and to be a doer. {Romans 10:14; James 1:22; John 6:45}

(2) Believing in order to have faith and be saved. {Hebrews 11:6; Mark 16:16}

(3) Repentance for forgiveness of sin; and in order to turn to goodness. Repentance is a direct command of God. It is a condition (not a deed) for forgiveness of sin. {Acts 2:38; Romans 2:4; Acts 17:30}

(4) Confession is an acknowledgement (witness) of your faith before mankind, God and the whole heavenly host. It is an act showing one's true colors to reveal one's true self without fear of shame. It is a confession unto salvation proclaiming that Jesus is the Son of God and the provider of salvation. {First Timothy 6:12; Romans 10:9, 10; Matthew 10:32, 33}

(5) Baptism is commanded by God. It is an immersion (burial) to wash away sins, get into Christ, and receive the gift of the

Holy Spirit within you. It is not a deed, it is an act of obedience and it gets you into the church that Christ established. It is for the forgiveness of sins in order to be saved. {Acts 10:48; Romans 6:3, 4 & Colossians 2:12; Acts 22:16; Galatians 3:26, 27; Acts 2:38; First Corinthians 12:13}

RetroClipArt.com

"By the authority of God, I baptize you for the forgiveness of sin in the Name of God the Father, God the Son, and God the Holy Ghost and you shall receive the gift of the Holy Spirit."
{Mark 16:16; Acts 2:38; Matthew 28:19}

Beyond these commands there is a whole host of directives from God that Christians must obey. There is love, worship, Christian living, evangelism, personal responsibility, and accountability as well as a number of things a Christian should not do.

Someone has said, *"Truth lies at the bottom of a well, the water of which serves as a mirror in which objects may be reflected."* As we seek truth let us be careful that we have not seen a distorted image created by ripples and adore it instead. The waters sometimes get stirred. One cannot understand or believe truth until he has acquired a foundation based upon the rational elimination of alternatives. One's resulting faith will then rest upon a foundation of sound reflections and will therefore command respect by those to whom he wishes to give witness of his belief.

12

TO KNOW GOD

RetroClipArt.com

"He tells us what we need to know!"

For some time now there are a great many people who are becoming secularists at heart but have been ashamed to admit their true position, even to themselves. They do not resist the ensuing eradication of established religious practices. They do not hold to the classical practices of their forefathers.

They may carry on nominal religious performances instead of having spiritual integrity and practicing heartfelt obedience toward God. Many may have abandoned real faith in God while they still pretend to be religious. Merely participating in ceremony or ritual, falls short of simple trust in God. God wants heartfelt obedience and commitment.

The solution for these people has been to practice what may be termed as a "mild religion" labeled under the guise of progressivism. Some may even participate in celebrations of emotional outbursts that provide them with moments of public expression to enjoy getting attention from others[41] without regard for the preferences of God.

Possibly, they appear to be searching momentarily for some new deity to provide their immediate wants. They seek to partake of the forbidden fruit that will provide their every desire immediately. These people hope to enlist some deity (or government) that will provide for their desires and serve them according to their wishes and guidelines.

It is interesting to note that many of these people are afraid to close the door on any possibility for the future. They have been afraid to oppose the love of God and withhold homage to Him entirely, even though they have been convinced that the idea of God is obsolete in their daily lives.

Some even take temporary visits in which they are enabled to feel good about themselves by making short-term ventures into the practice of Christianity. They may deliver a few holiday gifts to the needy or take a short mission trip into the under-developed neighborhoods. However, when one does this without taking any

[41] Or a luxurious state.

real risks involving an irrevocable commitment, their brief moment of piety seems to lack any traction.

There is a story of a young lady who left her sumptuous family home in the Beacon Hill section of Boston, Mass and dwelled among the inhabitants of one of the less fortunate neighborhoods. She became friends with another girl whose birthplace was in this section of town. One day when the girl from Beacon Hill was giving herself some accolades for living in this neighborhood, the other girl just starred at her in disbelief. Then she said: *"You can always go back up the hill, but I have no other place but here."*

Mild religion has seemed to be an innocuous middle ground; one ostensibly that is not against the historic Christian faith but, also, avoids any clear or definite commitment of obedience to God as He commands.

Because this situation is rapidly taking place in the Western World, I expect committed Christians to become a conscious minority, surrounded by a militant and arrogant paganism, which is the logical development of our secularist trend.

People must be led to see that our world is reaping consequences of a prolonged neglect comparable to that described in Judges 2:10. The prophet tells it like it is! *"And there arose another generation after them that knew not God . . ."*

When people fail to know God, the results on earth will always be the same: domestic discord, disobedient children, lawlessness, rebellion, sexual perversion, and disregard for God! Society's laissez-faire attitude toward civilized decent behavior adds to the complication. This is the picture of Romans 1:28-32. It exists now exactly as it existed then, and for the same reasons.

For the most part, we are living in a time where many people will not submit themselves to anyone, even for the common good. Family failures stand out in full evidence of this condition.

For whatever reason, there are those who will not allow themselves to be taught much of anything. Many are not only non-submissive; they behave in defiance to their own best interest. They are not amenable to the laws of man or God; they refuse to have even the first conception of God or His Word. They know nothing of sin or righteousness; are not responsible for their actions, and the Word of God is not known by them to even be addressed to them. Actually, it can be observed that those who have not the ability to believe have not the ability to disbelieve. They seem to simply exist in a "Neverland."

You cannot know the truth of God or His Will except as you have been taught it through the medium of His Word (Bible) which is the revelation of essential truth. God communicated what He wanted man to know and do; and that man might be informed as to one's duty to God.

God has revealed His Will through chosen persons. Such persons were not to teach more or less than God revealed. If they did, they were naïve to believe that they knew the mind of God without God's revealing such understandings.

Since man cannot know the mind of God on any subject, save as God has revealed it, you must understand why we are confined to the revelation as provided by God for man in the Bible.

Our understanding of God's will on all subjects pertaining to our life on earth, and the preparation necessary so that we may be with Him in our next life does not emanate from within us. We cannot go to heaven by a way that we devise. {Romans 6:17} Heaven is God's Home, and it is His right to say who shall share that Home with Him. Being confined to the Word of God for our knowledge of

God, and His Will concerning us, makes the importance of studying the Bible objectively apparent.

I dislike starting on such a fearful platform, but as Solomon said, *"The fear of the Lord is the beginning of knowledge."* {Proverbs 2:5} Now is the time to clear things up and make sure that we are traveling along the right path with our souls. A "fail-safe" policy is the best mode for the future.

It is better to heed warnings ahead of time, rather than letting ourselves default to a position of saying, *"I will never let that happen again."* An old saying in medicine is *"an ounce of prevention is worth a pound of cure."* Some preventable failures are very difficult to recover from.

13

PREPARATION FOR SESSIONS WITH GOD

RetroClipArt.com

"Who!"

Regardless of whom the president of the United States might be or which political party is in power, think about how awesome it might be to stand in the president's oval office in the White House before the president. This level of awe pales when compared to the emotion of mingled reverence, dread, and the wonder of standing in the conscious presence of God.

Before we approach God and ask who He is I want you to think further than before about whom you are and how you think that God and others really see you. Let's take a few moments to prepare for our first session with God. You could affect God's responses toward you.

Perhaps it is better to start with some real basics. The first thing to do is to look at yourself and find out who you really are, honestly. Yeah, I know, you're not there yet. You're still working on it. And you don't need someone else telling you what to do. Gosh, the typical psychologist says that you are what you are today because of something in your past or because something was left out, whichever. You could get that advice from Lucy in the Peanuts Gang for 5¢ along with a bop on the head (which could be more effective.) When people tell me to hang in there, I usually respond with *"I'm not hanging in there; my shirt-tail is caught and I'm being dragged along."* I just haven't made it yet, but I'm looking to God for my instructions and hoping He has a firm grip on my shirt-tail. Don't want to be like a story about Harvey:

> A fellow who was looking for a job stopped by a store to inquire about a friend named Harvey. The store owner told him that Harvey didn't work there anymore. The job seeker brightened. *"Well,"* he said, *"that means you have a vacancy." "Nope,"* said the store owner. *"Harvey didn't leave a vacancy. Everything around here is still the same. And when he left he said he wasn't going anywhere. I haven't seen him since he left here, either."*

Maybe Harvey found his nowhere. To live a lifetime and not leave a vacancy, to be present but not making any difference, is a distinct possibility. And it is indeed a dreadful epitaph for anyone. If this be you right now, then prepare to meet your God empty-handed, still naked like Adam and Eve when they tried to hide from God. You will be coming forth before Him. He will evaluate you and judge you.

Listen to God right now rather than your fellow-man, especially this author. Hand your crayon over to God right now. I trust that He is holding my crayon right now. Listen right on through the words that follow unto the very Words of God that He provides according to His Will, not yours, mine or anyone else. He speaks directly to you and me through His revelations found only when He chooses to speak through the people and means of His Choice, not yours, mine or any self-appointed authority.

God pointed out many years ago that the people in Berea were of more noble character than those in Thessalonica, for they received the message with all readiness of mind, and examined the Scriptures every day to see whether the things Paul said were true. {Acts 11:17} I doubt that Paul was considered by God, at this point in Paul's life, to be a false teacher. Rather, those in Berea must have been working on getting their understanding of what Paul said to be correct in their minds. They were developing within themselves their own understanding even after listening to Paul. We need teachers of truth to introduce truth, but we must work at getting the truth to hold within our minds. We are responsible directly to God for our own accountabilities. Essentially there are no intermediaries from God to us, just from us back to God through Jesus Christ. All Christians have become priests second only to the current High Priest, Jesus upon the elimination of the priesthood prior to Jesus. {Hebrews 7:11-17; 1 Peter 2:9}

Now is the time to fill your vacancy. You should listen to God and ask Him to decide for you rather than even trusting your own judgment. His Grace will be sufficient for you! {Second Corinthians 12:9} So let's invite God in here and stir things up a bit. Let the interview begin. (JR just said *"it's about time!"*)

14

SESSION 1: WHO ARE YOU GOD?

(A simulated interview)

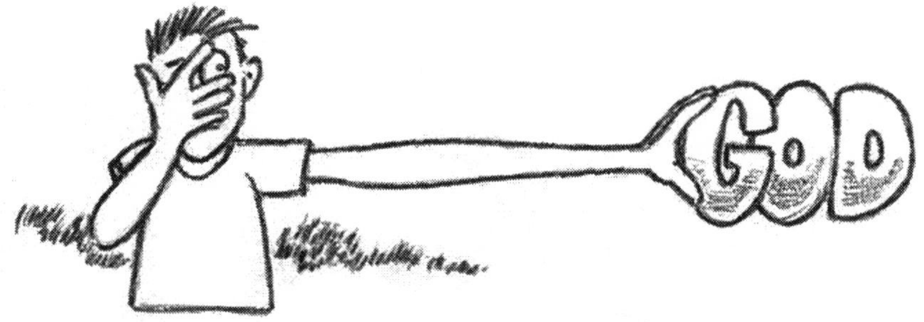

RetroClipArt.com

Warning: What you are about to read could make some of you angry with disbelief. Make sure that you are ready to think outside the box of your partisanship. You may need to examine some thoughts that are alien to your existing convictions. As your mind becomes more perceptive, you may become alienable to a new way of understanding God. You may find that the Word of God is clear and easy to understand. You could discover your nakedness before God. The realization of truth can set you free or it can be devastating. Such happenings can change who you are significantly. People who have known you in the past may not recognize you. You may become an alien to them. God's reality show can reveal our weaknesses and our destination. You may need to step out of the box you are in after you study and think outside the box where you reside now.

Note: Every word written in these sessions has been evaluated to determine that each word does not violate the integrity of the Bible. When words are presented as spoken by God they are written in ***Rockwell Extra Bold and italicized.***

Sometimes the author (Jim) inserts words to facilitate the effects of a conceptual narrative that expresses the author's perception of God's supposed, inferred, participation in this book. These inserts merely facilitate a feasible narrative with God as seen through the "mind's eye" of the author as reflected in the Bible. These words are not recorded directly in the Bible. In this book, these words are written in **Rockwell Extra Bold,** but are not *italicized.*

The author's words are written in **Arial Rounded M Bold**.

Occasionally: Rather than speak for God, the author shares his thoughts within the moment of context. These thoughts are expressions of the author as a mere mortal being with normal limited capacity as a human being (a man's viewpoint rather than God's.) Please do not view them as the direct Word of God. These thoughts of the author are written in ***Arial Rounded M Bold and are italicized whenever they occur during the dialogue.***

Sometimes: Other friends of the author, much like Job's friends, jump into the scene seemingly unaware of the Presence of God. Thomas is the most outspoken of these friends. He is somewhat like the Apostle Thomas who is known to doubt a thing or two and likes to see proof. {John 20:25} Along the way, Thomas responds to explanations positively proving that he listens. Occasionally, others will jump into the scene. The author tends to respond to his friends' intrusions without bothering God. So far, no lightening-strikes have occurred as warnings to the author or his friends. The words of the author's friends are written in Comic Sans MS.

The author is hereafter referred to as "Jim."

RetroClipArt.com

Scene: There are two chairs with a table between the chairs. A copy of the Bible lies on the table and there is a stream of sunlight flowing through a window shown about the Bible as a solid arch or vault. The vault is surrounded by a magnificent dispersion of colors created by portions of the sunlight passing through trees just outside the window and the prism effect of the window panes. Jim is circumspectly sitting in one chair and the other chair appears to be empty. The Bible is open to Psalm 8. Seemingly to pass the time, thinking that he is waiting on God, Jim reads Psalm 8 as it is plainly in his view. Jim feels good about the coming interview as Psalm 8 reveals that God cares for people. Suddenly there is a soft breath of fresh air in the room like one would feel upon opening a window in the freshness of springtime. Jim looks around for a couple of minutes, enjoying the pleasantness of the moment. Then, as if to disrupt the splendor Jim thinks, seemingly to the world, ***I don't see God. I hope He shows up.*** But then as he reads on into the 9th Psalm, where we are reminded in verse 10 that God will not forsake those who seek Him, Jim seems to hear God talking.

God: **Hello Jim!**

Jim: **God, is that You?**

God: **Yes Jim!**

Jim: **Where are You God? I don't see You.**

God: **I'm right here Jim. How would you like Me to appear?**

Jim: **I just want to see You in person.**

God: **You know I won't allow that right now.**

Jim: **Why?**

God: **My first response is similar to what your mother used to say, "Just because I said so, I am your mother. That's why." Of course, I am not your fleshly mother, but I always have the FINAL WORD. You can always depend on My Words right on through the end of time into eternity and beyond. I am Sovereign and My Words are Final, without exception. I am the Creator and the Owner of everything that exists. I have the power and authority over angels, men, and all creation. All things begin with Me and My Will prevails forever. I am the Almighty!** {Genesis 1:1; Psalm 135:5-6; Daniel 4:34-35; Psalm 24:1; Acts 14:15; Acts 17:24-28; Revelation 4:8-11; 1:8} **Even the devils know who I am.** {James 2:19} **Why do you have trouble understanding this?**

Jim: Hum, guess I don't know.

God: **Just think about it Jim. What personification would you like for Me to embody? Would you think of yourself as being in My likeness if I appeared in some color other than yours? Do you perceive Me to be tall or short? Right now your spirit is contained in your carnal habitat, clothed within a human body. I am not. I have no carnal form even though I could appear in any form I choose. I am not clothed in earthly flesh like you. In your human language I am Spirit.** {John 4:24} **I gave you a spirit like Mine that is a soul, when I breathed the**

breath of life into you. You became a living soul. {Genesis 2:7}

Jim, thinking: *Our soul is our distinct entity apart from our carnal bodies. The body is simply a "container" for our spirit. The soul is the animating principle providing us with the facilities of thought, action, and emotion and held to be separable in existence; the spiritual part of humans as distinct from the human body. It is in the image of God as a spirit. It is our succession from our human life. It does not perish along with our human body at death. While our bodies are mortal our spirit is immortal. The Holy Spirit bears witness with our spirits that we are children, of God, therefore co-heirs with Christ in His glory.* {Romans 8:16} *Our soul has a heart just as God has a heart.* {Acts 13:22} *This heart is the central, vital, or main part or core of our soul; separate and distinct from the muscular organ that circulates the blood in our human bodies by alternate dilation and contraction. Your spiritual heart is the core of your soul. It is the center of emotions, personality, attributes, and the uniqueness of you. It provides your inmost thought, feeling, love, sympathy, courage, and reactions. Your mind of the spirit serves as the consciousness for your soul. Yes, your soul has a mind. This is correct; within your personal spirit is a mind. It is the seat of consciousness. Your mind is the liaison between your human body and your soul. It is facilitated by your brain where human imaging and reasoning takes place; along with control of your bodily functions. [Just check this out in a dictionary.] God helps us understand this clearly as He says: "And he who searches our hearts knows the mind of the Spirit, because the Spirit intercedes for the saints in accordance with God's Will."* {Romans 8:27} *"O Jerusalem, wash the evil from your heart and be saved. How long will you harbor wicked thoughts?"* {Jeremiah 4:14} *"For out of the heart come evil thoughts, murder, adultery, sexual immorality, theft, false testimony, slander."* {Matthew 15:19}

God continues: **When your body dies it will become dust and return to the ground it came from. Your soul will return to Me.** {Ecclesiastes 12:7}

Jim, thinking: *Wow! This means the real me is eternal and my soul will exist into eternity beyond the death of my body. Guess there is no option for me to drop out. I am stuck with myself. Dr. Seuss*[42] *once said "Today you are You, that is truer than true. There is no one alive who is Youer than you."*

God: **Careful Jim, you sound good but you must understand what you are saying. You can't just talk your way into My eternal home. Your knowledgeable, conscious choices will determine where you stay. Your soul is eternal but it will either go away into everlasting punishment or life eternal with Me, at My Home in Heaven.** {Matthew 25:46}

Jim: No problem. I have decided to choose heaven.

---

[42] See footnote 12. This is another one of his many popular quotes.

God: **That's a great choice, but you must understand that whether or not you get in depends upon whether you know Me and obey the Gospel of My Son, Jesus Christ.** {Second Thessalonians 8-10}

God continues: **That is all up to you. You do have control of your future through making the right choices. You just don't have control of the results of your choices. Why do you struggle with this? It would be like changing the natural laws such as gravity. Can you really change any of these? I can if I want to, but you cannot do so. You are only free to make choices. You cannot make or change the consequences. I am 100% in charge and you are 100% responsible for your choices.**

Jim: This is hard to see.

God: **Jim, what's with this seeing thing? Surely you can understand such elementary thoughts. Can you see your spirit? Your spirit is not visible to the human eye. You will be able to see Me in the future when you appear before Me in your new spiritual body. That new body is not physical.** {Second Corinthians 5:1-10} **It will be perfect.**

Jim: You spent time with Adam and Eve in the Garden of Eden.

God: **Yes Jim, I used to visit in the garden with Adam and Eve when there was no sin on earth. They had no need for clothes as they were not affected by being naked. In the beginning they had no knowledge of good and evil. They were totally innocent of any wrong doing because they had done no wrong. When they disobeyed Me by eating from the forbidden tree they became knowledgeable of good and evil. They lost their innocence and became liable for sin. They suddenly realized that they were naked and were ashamed. They no longer held the innocence of a small child who can run naked through a room of strangers without embarrassment. They initially sewed fig leaves together and made coverings for themselves. They hid from Me when they heard me coming. Then I made garments of skin and clothed them. I expelled them from the garden as punishment and as an act of mercy. If they were to eat of the tree of life they would live forever in a state of death and alienation.** {Genesis 3:1-24}

God continues: **I would not be able to return them into My Presence. I just can't allow sin to exist in My Presence. I am of purer eyes than to behold evil, and I cannot look on wickedness.** {Habakkuk 1:13} **As long as you are tainted by sin you cannot enter My Presence or see Me. The view**

of such perfect righteousness by human eyes would destroy you. It would be like looking directly at the sun on a clear day. Your carnal eyes cannot look directly at the sun. The full-brightness of the sun would destroy your eyes. No one can see My Face and live. {Exodus 33:20} **So I am keeping some distance between you and Me right now in order to protect you. I am reframing from letting you see Me right now. I must remain imperceptible to you for a while. You can have a good look at Me when you appear before Me for your final judgment. I will appear visibly as Myself when Jesus presents you before Me without fault.** {Jude 24-25} **You will be able to perceive Me then. Jim, you can see Me later.** {Revelation 22:3-4}

God continues: **Besides, My Son has already visited earth and represented Me among people for a while. He became flesh in order to make Me known to you.** {John 1:1-18} **Those who saw Him have seen the essence of Me.** {John 14:7-9} **He was My virtual image.** {Colossians 1:15, Hebrews 1:3} **He is the only way to Me.** {John 14:7-9} **He carried out My plan for your salvation and enabled your return to My Presence. He took away sin for you. He removed the barrier between you and Me.** {First John 3:5} **(I'll say more about that later.)**

Jim: I believe there were witnesses to the presence of Jesus on earth. I don't doubt they saw Jesus. But I need to see You for myself to be sure. I have difficulty grasping a form of God on earth as a human. Just give me a sign.

God: **What? Must I repeat Myself? I allowed John a view into part of heaven but he never saw Me directly in this vision.** {Book of Revelation}

Jim, thinking: *Oops! I don't think that was a good idea on my part. Maybe, I should not doubt His Word. He seems to have stated the terms of His Offer of a relationship with mankind. I don't think He is willing to negotiate at all.*

God continues: **Until you receive your new body you will just have to accept the present conditions. I cannot allow sin in My presence. As I just said, Adam and Eve realized this when they hid from Me in the Garden of Eden. They were embarrassed because they realized that they were naked; thus, revealing their sinful nature which is forbidden before Me. Now only the holy, sinless angels and Jesus are in My presence.** {Luke 1:19} **I sent the Holy Spirit to be with you.** {John 7:37-39; Galatians 4:6; First Corinthians 3:16}

Jim: This is just so complicated.

God: **Jim, you brought up Dr. Seuss in your thoughts. Dr. Seuss also said "Sometimes the questions are complicated and the answers are simple." Actually, you don't need the questions when you have the answers. I have**

provided you with the answers. This is not a reverse engineering dialog. Just follow the answers. They are clear. You can do all of them within the boundaries of My Grace and Mercy. They are self-sufficient in explanation for your understanding. Dr. Seuss, also, stated "I said what I meant and I meant what I said." To you and Dr. Seuss, I say "Me too." There you be, Jim. Take My Word for it. Didn't your Papa Jim say that to you, also, several times!

Time-out: Jim appears to be grappling with his words now. He seems to be startled with God's answers. God's answers are so plain and simple they are disarming Jim's control of the interview. It is as if Jim expected different answers. Jim can't seem to find any viable contrasting viewpoints to what God has to say. God's Words are compelling beyond refutation. God does have the Final Word. However, Jim does not cease asking questions. His insatiable appetite for truth and security summons more questions. He does not appear daunted in his pursuit for the truth.

Jim, thinking: ***I believe that most of us are looking for some sort of rescue where we can feel safe. Bill Crowder43 expressed this well in one of his devotional writings as he reflected on the 2013 movie Man of Steel. This movie was a fresh imagining of the Superman comic book story that many of us enjoyed during our days of youth. The new release was filled with breath-taking special***

[43] Bill Crowder is one of the authors of *Our Daily Bread*, a daily devotional booklet published by RBC Ministries. (Now known as Our Daily Bread Ministries.) This reference is found in the February 24, 2015 entry.

effects and nonstop action. Huge crowds around the world turned out to see this release. Some said the film's appeal came from the amazing technology used in the making of this movie. Others pointed to the enduring lure of the "Superman mythology." Bill pointed out that Amy Adams, the actress who plays Lois Lane in the movie, has a different view of Superman's appeal. She says it is about a basic human longing for rescue. She says, "Who doesn't want to believe there's one person who could come and save us from ourselves." I saw an image of Superman on the screen, myself. Because I have seen an image of Superman he sometimes seems real to me. This image personifies a real hero to me who could protect me from all harm. I sometimes wonder why so many of us continue to watch strife as it is displayed on television and in movies. I am beginning to realize that we really do want to see the good guys triumph over the bad guys. We may not find our enjoyment in the demonstration of violence. Rather, we see the purveyors of strife being destroyed. This provides us with a feeling of safeness. We do want to see evil eliminated. However, these images are not real. They exist only virtually. It is natural for humans to want to see a favorable image even if it is only a vision. Somehow, we struggle with faith as it requires that we trust without seeing anything familiar. We want to witness the rescuer in person. Faith is impossible to see and difficult to comprehend. It has no visibility. It is the substance of things hoped for, not seen. It is void of any physical matter. I just don't always have a good feeling about faith. Sometimes I have no confidence in my ability to discern such phenomenon. I struggle with things unusual.

Jim: I just need to feel your presence.

God: **Awe, there's your problem. You have lost your "sense" of My Presence. Yes, your sins have separated you from Me. You can make Me angry because of your sin, but you must understand that I gave you the gift of the Holy Spirit when you were baptized for the forgiveness of your sins. You have the presence of Me within yourself by virtue of the indwelling Holy Spirit.** {John 14:23; 15:4} **That indwelling presence comes only through faith and your acts of obedience to My Word. Baptism is an act of obedience wherein I come into your presence within you through the Holy Spirit entering into you and dwelling there.** {Acts 2:38-39} **Baptism washes away your sins.** {Acts 22:16} **It is for the forgiveness of sins.** {Acts 2:38} **I commanded it.** {Acts 10:48} **Jesus did it. He was sinless, but He did it anyway to fulfill all righteousness. He was an example for everyone. I was pleased with Him.** {Matthew 3:13-17} **Why do you choose to doubt My Word? Do you believe anything you did not witness yourself?**

Jim, thinking: *Jesus was a good example. God did say that sin separates us from Him. Guess that some of us have been a bit stubborn on that one. Baptism looks simple and reasonable to me. It just seems that I always want to be different. I just don't like being told what to do. But the cost seems modest and the potential payoffs do appear to be attractive. The alternatives appear to be devastating. Again, maybe, I should not doubt His Word. He still does not seem ready to negotiate with me at all. Guess I have no alternative but to comply with God's directives.*

God continues: **After Jesus completed His work on earth and returned home to sit on My Right Side I chose to maintain a relationship between you and Me based on faith derived from the testimonies of those I choose to speak on My behalf, including my Son, Jesus Christ, Who spoke the Gospel. You can find what you need to know in the teachings of Jesus and the Apostles. The rest is mostly for your historical knowledge, guidance, and warning. That's it, no more and no less so. You can't change it, just heed it. All that's necessary for you to know is right here in the Bible. I worded the Bible, so I should know.** {Second Timothy 3: 16-17}

God continues: **Therefore, you must recognize Me through faith. Otherwise, there is no need for faith. After Jesus became the sacrifice for the forgiveness of your sins, I chose faith and baptism as the gateway through which you must enter My Presence. I am sovereign**

so I determine these matters. The choice is not yours. Simply believe that I am, seek Me and I will find you. {Hebrews 11:6} **I will give you everything you need for life and godliness.** {Second Peter 1:3-4} **There is no need for a manual.** {Second Timothy 3:16, 17}

God continues: **Michael Angelo took a perceptive likeness pass on the fleshly body of my Son, Jesus. But Michael never saw My Son. I don't want you to worship a worldly image in any form or likeness. An image can become an idol. You must worship Me and My Son in spirit and in truth.** {John 4:23-24} **You must have faith in Me** {Mark 11:22; Hebrews 11:6} **and My Son.** {John 14:1; 8:24}

Jim, thinking: *Faith is being sure about what one has not personally seen. If we believed the paintings were real images we would probably begin to worship the physical paintings. God does not want that to happen. The paintings have no power.*

God continues: **After I ran Adam and Eve out of the garden I appeared in forms of My choosing to Abraham, Moses, Isaac, Jacob and, later, to others as I began to establish my covenant people and begin the broad strokes of My plan of redemption (rescue) for mankind. They all recognized My presence without doubt. They remained fairly calm. None of them showed any outbursts of uncontrolled emotions**

during these encounters. This should tell you that I could appear in some recognizable normal forms when I so choose. But I have never appeared in a human recognizable, exact image of Myself. There are no valid recognizable pictures or recordings. I have not appeared on earth in the legitimate imagination of an artist. For an artist it would be like painting a violent wind without superficial images. {Acts 2:2}

God continues: **The common aspect about all my visits with humans has been that they heard Me speak. Adam certainly heard Me clearly. When I spoke to Moses from a burning bush, he hid his face because he was afraid to look at Me.** {Exodus 3:1-6}

Jim, thinking: *Hum, guess he didn't want to be destroyed—good thinking Moses.*

God continues: **But he did hear and understand Me. Jim, while you are carnal I will speak to you through My WORD which is found in the Bible before you. It does not tell everything, but it is all you need to know for obeying Me now.** {Second Timothy 3:16} **I have more to say to you, but any more would be more than you can bear now. It was given by Me through inspiration to My chosen writers. It is My Final Word, not those of the writers. It does not require**

one's own interpretation. {Second Peter 1:20-21} **You should not change it or add to it.** {Revelation 22:18-19} **What you say is not what I say. If you were omnipotent as I am then your word would rule. No one is absolutely sovereign but Me.** {Revelation 11:17}

Jim: Your Words in the Bible seem somewhat out of sync with the times.

God: **Jim, the times are what are out of sync. Evidently some people are throwing you into confusion and trying to pervert the Gospel of My Son, Jesus Christ.** {Galatians 1:6-9}

Jim: The Bible is so hard to interpret. I need an expert to tell me what You said and what it should mean to me.

God: **Jim, I just told you that I did not even allow the chosen writers to make their own interpretation. It does not require an interpretation.** {Again, Second Peter 1:20} **I mean exactly what I say. You must handle My Word correctly yourself.** {Second Timothy 2:15; Acts 17:11} **I talk to you with Words that you can understand. Why would I do otherwise? My Word is only a mystery to those who don't listen very closely. Sometimes I use metaphors to help you understand by referring to something you recognize as, essentially, the same in purpose or action. As I speak to you I say what**

I mean and mean what I say. Why would I do otherwise if I am trying to communicate with you?

God continues: **Philip helped the Ethiopian understand what he was reading in the book of Isaiah. Philip taught him about the good news of Jesus that Isaiah was talking about and baptized him.** {Acts 8:26-39} **He did not provide the eunuch with a private interpretation. He explained what it said.** {Second Peter 1:20} **My Spirit took Philip away and the eunuch went on his way rejoicing. Apparently the Ethiopian eunuch understood My Word as explained through Philip clearly and reacted accordingly. Jim, you can do the same as the eunuch. Just listen to My Words throughout all the scriptures so that you can buttress your understanding of My Words.**

Jim, thinking: *Hum, which does make sense.*

God continues: **The reason you do not follow me with understanding is because you want Me to say what pleases you. I won't do that. I am God and you are not. It is time for you to listen to what I have to say with an understanding and a faith that results in an attitude of love and actions of trust and obedience. There is no other way whereby you can be saved.** {Galatians 1:8-9; Acts 4:12} **Take My Word and abide by**

it with trust and dependency. Don't quibble with Me.

Jim: Okay God. I get it. You are participating in this interview through the Bible right in front of me here on the table, aren't You? How did you do that to me? I began reading Psalm 8 and You have been responding to my thoughts through Your Holy Words. That's amazing. I can get really caught up with You through my presence in Your Holy Words as provided in the Bible. You have answered all my questions from within the Bible.

Jim, thinking: *This is a great feeling! And it is not a fantasy. I suspect that Thomas is feeling vindicated about now. I am pleased to realize that I can carry on a conversation with God right in the Bible. I can pose a question and God waits patiently while I search for His answers in the Bible. In addition, He stays open for my prayers. After all, what good would prayer be if God would not listen to us? We may not always like His answers, but that's the way it is. So we must carry on. It's doable.*

God: **That's right Jim. It's all right there for those who hear, understand, and submit their will to My Will. My Grace will be sufficient for all who are obedient** {Second Corinthians 12:9} **to all that I have commanded in the Bible. That means every word in My Words before and after all conjunctions. You can't just select a few phrases at your pleasure. You must comprehend the whole in its entirety.**

God continues: **I have provided direct commands, examples in the early congregations in the times of the Apostles, and I left some things in the form of necessary inference, but with guidance in the form of principles for your behavior. If you just follow the good examples of the early Christians and heed the warnings I gave them as found in the New Testament you will do just fine. There is no need to change or add anything. It is not required and I really like doing it My Way. If you were Me, wouldn't you prefer the same?**

Jim: Yes!

God: **The Bible was given by Me through inspiration to My chosen writers that you might know all you need to know.** {John 16:13}

Jim: Okay. I will take a timeout here. You're in charge. I'll wait until you are ready. I'll just stare around here somewhere.

RetroClipArt.com

Burning Bush

God: **Jim, what would you like? Do you want a plague? Don't push me or I will speak to you in the wilderness from a burning bush where I can place you at My Will or make you into a perch for some locusts or put you in the mouth of a big fish. Just listen to Me and I will tell you what you need to know. Don't worry about images, just focus on hearing and understanding My Words. Don't delete or add anything. Study carefully. Respect My Words. Then obey all of My Words.** {Acts 17:11; Hebrews 2:1-4; First Corinthians 4:6; Second Corinthians 4:2; Revelation 22:18-19; James 1:22-27}

Jim: Okay God! I don't mean to offend you. I just want to get it right. Even if you send it to me through the horse's mouth I will listen. Do you want me to stand, sit, or bow down?

God: **Well, I am God you know. If you were Me (that is if you were in My place you would be God) what would you expect from mankind? Would you allow them to do as they please without consequences? Would you let them dictate to you? How would you feel when they disobey you? Would you be pleased with them?**

Jim: No, of course not. I just think that it would be nice if You provided visible leadership and destroyed all of our enemies and eliminated our problems. It would make it easier for us to follow You. Life is tough here on earth.

God: **Jim, I have always provided the necessary guidance for life on earth. I did it with Adam and Eve. I warned Adam and Eve ahead of time.** {Genesis 2:17} **I did not sneak up on them with surprises. I have provided mankind with guidance and warnings from the very beginning of mankind in the Garden of Eden, through the Law of Moses, the Patriarchs, some Priests, the Judges, some Kings, the Prophets, the Apostles, the Bible along with the assistance of the Holy Spirit, and most of all, My Son Jesus Christ. Just like Adam and Eve, it is so difficult for you to accept Me as I am. You just don't follow My Words. That's the problem.** {Bible as a whole}

Time-out: Like many people, Jim becomes discombobulated in the presence of such compelling thoughts. He momentarily loses his concentration.

Jim: Sorry, what's Your point, again?

God: **Loving obedience, plain and simple. I prefer obedience over sacrifice.** {First Samuel 15:22}

Jim, thinking: *Oops, He said that again. I was thinking of a gift offering of some of my best stuff. Maybe I need to change the subject.*

Jim: I thought it was all about love, mercy, and grace?

God: **Yes, Jim. It is about My love for you and your love for Me. It is a mutual relationship. If you loved Me you would do what I say because you love Me. Because I love you I am willing to provide mercy and grace when you repent of your sins and obey Me in all truth, including baptism for the remission of your sins whereby I give you the gift of the Holy Spirit and free you from the effects of sin.** {Acts 2:38} **Jim, you are the one who sinned, not Me. Sin is what separates you and Me.** {Isaiah 59:1-2} **You remind me of the kid with cookie crumbs in the corners of his mouth saying "who me?" when his mother inquired about the missing cookies. I should have let Adam name man as the "ostrich."**

Jim: Well, I'm no ostrich and I do have a brain.

God: **Jim, you only think you know Me. If you really knew Me you would love Me by keeping My Commandments.** {First John 2:30} **My greatest Commandment to you is to "Love the Lord your God with all your heart and with all your soul and with all your mind."** {Matthew 22:37-38} **When you commit your heart and soul to love it should be natural for your mind to follow my instructions. I first loved you. I showed My love for you in creation and I sent My Son as an atoning sacrifice for your sins.** {First John 4:9-12} **My love has always provided mankind with clear life-sustaining instructions. Mankind should consummate our Love for each other through an obedience driven by My love within the hearts of mankind. I am Love.** {First John 4:7-8}

God continues: **Adam and Eve failed to follow my instructions and look what happened to them. Adam had a nice job that I gave him. I gave him a wife to be his natural companion. I enjoyed each and every day of creation. It was good because everything I created did what it was supposed to do in the beginning. That's why each day I gazed upon My creations of the day and described them as "good."** {Genesis 1, 2}

Jim, thinking: ***Oops, I think He's about to repeat Himself, again. Guess He really considers this important. I think He must be ticked off with mankind.***

God continues: **I spoke with Adam several times. I gave Adam specific instructions about the tree of knowledge of good and evil. I told him that if he ate from this tree he would die.** {Genesis 2:16-17} **Adam and Eve simply blew it all away. They chose disobedience as their course of action, and I chose mine. They let Satan deceive them. Satan led them into sin.** {Genesis 3:1-6} **They believed a lie instead of trusting Me. As a Holy God, I could respond only in a way consistent with My perfect moral nature. I could not allow sin to go un-checked; I had to cut-off those who do it. Just as I banished the fallen angels from heaven, I separated mankind from my immediate presence. The wages of sin had to be exacted.** {Romans 6:23} **All sinners are cut off from My source of life.** {Ephesians 4:18} **I am the source of all life, you know. Now everyone dies through Adam.** {First Corinthians 15:21-22} **Death spread to all mankind because everyone sins.** {Romans 5:12} **People have become the children of the devil rather than belonging to Me.** {John 8:42-47}

Jim: That's really extreme for a first offense!

RetroClipArt.com

"Death?"

God: **Remember that their sin set in motion the world's tendency toward disobeying Me. One of the realities of sin is that its effects spread. After Eve sinned, she involved Adam in her wrong doing. You should have seen the two of them covered with fig leaves trying to hide from Me. It would have been humorous if were not so devastating. How could they be so silly as to think they could actually hide from Me? Adam and Eve created the barrier that separates them from Me. They brought into existence the shame and embarrassment which caused them to hide from Me. I will provide grace and mercy to those who confess and repent before Me in absolute nakedness voluntarily without capture along with complete obedience to My commands.**

I do not hold mankind hostage on earth, so that all people have choices. Mankind is held hostage by sin. Death came into existence in order that sin might be recognized as sin. Sin is the primary problem, rather than death. {Romans 8: 7-25}

Jim, thinking: *God seems to be heating up. I need to be careful. Death is God's direct reaction against man's sin. Death results from God's abandoning of the people who abandoned Him first. If Adam and Eve had eaten of the Tree of Life they would have escaped death and lived forever in their human form. But then God provided a plan of redemption for mankind back into His eternal presence and safety. Sin brought on death because death is separation from the breath of life with comes directly from God. Therefore, mankind separated ourselves from God as we see Adam and Eve hiding in the Garden of Eden right after their disobedience.*

Jim: I thought obedience was the problem. Now it looks more like sin is the major problem. Maybe I misunderstand what sin is. What does sin mean to You, God?

God: **Jim. Now you are thinking. Obedience and sin are opposites. They are contradictory. Sin is disobedience to My Will. Failure to adhere to My Holy Commandments is sin. You have transgressed My Law.** {First John 3:4-12} **My laws define how you demonstrate love to Me and your fellowman.** {Deuteronomy 30: 15-16} **All**

unrighteousness is sin. {First John 5:17} **Failure to do good that I have commanded is sin.** {James 4:17} **Anything not of faith is sin. To do anything that you doubt that I approve of is sin.** {Romans 14:23} **Therefore, disobedience is sin and I cannot allow sin in My presence. In effect, they are one in the same. When you are disobedient to My commandments you miss the mark of righteousness that I have set for you, and that is sin.**

Jim: Looks like I have some clear choices I need to make in regards to how I will conduct my life on earth.

God: **Jim, that's right. When your human life dies your opportunity to make choices stops completely. You were purchased with the blood of My Son Jesus. When you die you are Mine again and I will do with you what pleases Me. You will be finished with your turn. You need to heed My Words as you make choices while you still have an opportunity to do so.**

Jim: All of them?

God: **Yes! Don't you understand conjunctions and comprehensive instructions? Don't be like the ostrich, sticking your head in the sand. Look around at all My Words. My commands are not optional. Heed all of them.**

Jim, thinking: *God seems sad at the moment.*

Jim: God, you seem sad now.

God: **I became saddened when people chose sin instead of a relationship with Me; that is Eve and everyone that followed.** {Genesis 6:5-7} **I had just about given up with My creation of man until Noah came along.** {Genesis 6:8-9} **That man followed my instructions in every detail without question or alteration. So I decided to allow mankind along with the other living creatures a fresh start, but I had to find a way to redeem everybody. All mankind needs to be rescued.**

Jim: God, you know that many people simply do not believe that things like the flood, parting of the sea, Jonah, etc. really happened. Evil is not real to many. Demons and devils have become fictitious characters for amusement and entertainment. They see all of this as fictional stories or as natural happenings rather than supernatural acts of Yours. They may see deceivers as friends in need of understanding and help. Some do not see any real enemies anywhere.

God: **Jim, that's their problem. My struggle with man has always been the same. In fact, My Son, Jesus had to instruct His Disciples to depart from people who would not receive them or listen to their words and shake off**

the dust of their feet as they departed. {Matthew 10:14} **My Words are truth and they shall not pass away.** {Mark 13:31} **Sin has always been the problem. I just can't accept it at all.**

God continues: **Besides I have been irritated with battling demons that are not flesh and blood, over which Satan has control. I have limited Satan's schemes and the powerful forces of fallen angels headed by Satan, who is a vicious fighter. That devil is still your enemy and he is looking to devour you.** {Job 1:6-2:8 and First Peter 5:8}

Jim, thinking: *I wish God had not allowed Satan on earth while I am here.*

God continues: **The devil has been stepping up his persecution because he knows that his time is short.** {Revelation 12:12} **I revealed My conflict with Satan in chapters 12 – 14 in the book of Revelation. Learn every one of these Words of Mine so that you will know who the enemy is and how dangerous he is to you.**

Jim, thinking: *He's getting a bit riled, maybe I need to change the subject again.*

But, God continues: **I revealed to John the source of all sin, evil, persecution, and suffering on earth. John saw why the great battle with the**

forces of Satan must take place. In the Book of Revelation the nature of evil is exposed, and Satan is seen in all his wickedness. Originally Satan was an angel of mine, but through his own pride he became corrupt. I did not create him evil. In fact, I have never created anything that is not good, beautiful and true. Satan turned evil on his own after I created him. Whether in heaven or on earth, every facet of creation, was originally "very good." {Genesis 1:31}

Time-out: God waits for Jim to finish his thinking.

Jim, thinking: *The Apostle Paul said it clearly: "Everything God created is good."* {First Timothy 4:4} *The character of the Creator is entirely pure; there isn't a shred of darkness within him.* {First John 1:5 and First Peter 2:4} *He did not create anything that was not good, even the devil. As the source of all goodness, beauty, and truth, God creates only what is consistent with His Nature. That is, God creates only things that are good, beautiful, and true. While on a working trip in Saudi Arabia one of my Arabian associates asked me "if the chicken or the egg came first?" I told him that God created the chicken and man laid the egg. He agreed with a laugh. The egg can become a chicken, but only the chicken can make an egg. An egg may simply become rotten if left on its own without an incubator. The Laws of God are that simple. They must be followed so that which begins as good may stay good. A sculptor was once asked how he sculpted an elephant.*

He said that he removed everything that did not look like an elephant. This suggests that we may have a few things that need removing from our lives so that we become what we should be.

Then God goes full-speed at {Revelation 12:7}: **Once upon a time there was a great war in heaven. Michael and his angels fought against Satan and his angels. Michael defeated them and drove them out of heaven down to earth. Satan and his angels are leading the whole world astray now.** Then God moves to {Genesis 3:1}: **Disguised as a crafty serpent Satan led Eve astray. Satan tempted Eve by getting her to doubt My Goodness. He implied that I was strict, stingy, and selfish for not wanting Eve to share My Knowledge of good and evil. He made Eve forget all that I had given her and, instead, focus on the one thing she could not have. Adam did not hesitate to join Eve in this move into infamy.**

God is on a roll and continues moving ahead at {Matthew 2:13-15}: **Satan used Herod in an attempt to destroy Jesus as a baby.** Then at {Matthew 4:11}: **Satan had the gall to tempt Jesus. Jesus did not sin.** Then continuing back to Revelation 12: **Jesus proceeds to defeat Satan through the shedding of His Blood for the sins of those who believe and obey His Gospel. Jesus was raised from the dead.** {Romans 6:9} **He holds the keys of death**

and Hades. {Revelation 1:18} **However, Satan still has power to deceive just as he did with Eve. Now he is battling Me on earth by tempting all humanity away from Me and My Son Jesus. Satan is filled with fury as he knows his time to take you in his army for the final battle is short. Don't let him get you. Satan will not have the winning side.** {Revelation 12:10-17}

God continues: **When Satan[44] became the prince of demons** {Matthew 12:24-28 and Mark 3:22} **he became My enemy and he constantly tries to hinder My Work to rescue mankind even though he is limited because of My Greater Power and can do only what I have permitted him to do.** {Job 1:6-2:8} **The name Satan means "accuser."** {Revelation 12:10} **He actively looks for people to attack.** {Job 1:7}

Jim: Why didn't You already cast Satan into hell fire? Why put up with him at all? Why did you create Satan?

Jim, thinking: *Do you think my questions are getting too inappropriate? Just think about not knowing about these realities at all! We become easy targets for Satan with his deceptions.*

God: **Well Jim, you do ask questions that quicken one's core being. The answer is not exactly complicated. Satan and all those**

[44] Aliases: The devil, Lucifer, Beelzebub.

who do not obey me are awaiting the Day of Judgment. Simply, the Day of Judgment still resides in the future. In fact, hell was created for Satan and his angels. In addition to man, the fallen angels will appear before the bar of judgment. Since they could not remain in My presence I cast them to earth for the time being along with Satan, who roams through the earth seeking whom he can devour. {First Peter 5:8}

Jim: Why did You create evil?

God: **I didn't create evil or sin. Evil is not a "thing" like a rock or man. You cannot have a jar of evil. Evil has no existence of its own; it is really the absence of good. I did allow evil to happen. If I had not allowed for the possibility of evil, both mankind and angels would be serving Me out of obligation, not choice. I did not want you to be My "robot" that I controlled like a puppet. I allowed the possibility of evil and sin so you could have a free will and choose whether or not you wanted to serve Me and survive with My Protection forever. I did not cause evil to exist. Satan and the rest of you brought that on yourselves through disobedience.**

Time-out: Jim hears his friend Thomas approaching.

Jim: Here comes my friend Thomas.

God: **Good. You talk with him now. You can come back to Me tomorrow. Thomas needs to hear about Me from you. He's not sure about some critical issues. The whole world needs to hear the truth. I need you to do just as Jesus commissioned the eleven (Judas was dead at that time) disciples: teach obedience to My Word to everyone. Remember that I will always be with you.** {Matthew 28:16-20}

15

AN INTERMISSION CONVERSATION WITH THOMAS

(Simulated)

RetroClipArt.com

Scene: As Thomas walks into the room Jim looks up from the Bible.

Thomas: Jim, who where you talking with?

Jim: **I was visiting with God.**

Thomas: Come on Jim. That's surrealistic. It's bizarre. That's just a fantasy of your wandering mind. You are dreaming again. It can't be real.

Jim: **Thomas, you are so fixed with your beliefs (understandings) that I am surprised that you ever learned how to do anything. Sometimes I cannot picture you as a baby, because if you were once a baby you could not have developed into who you are now. Did you attend walking school or did you walk right out of your mother's womb?**

Thomas: Now Jim. Be nice. You need to be "politically correct" these days. You need to conform to the ways that are acceptable where you live and with those of us who are your friends.

Thomas continues: Rich[45] talked you into doing this goofy thing, too, didn't he. He talked you into writing this silly book. No one will believe that you had an interview with God. You are wasting your time.

Time-out: Thomas sits down in the other chair. He appears troubled as he turns his head downward and stares at the floor.

Jim, thinking: ***Does Thomas really care? Why does he bother to even come around and speak to me? I think that he does care. He is just being aggressive because he is struggling with life, like many of us. If he didn't care***

[45] Rich is the friend who encouraged me to write this book.

he would probably ignore me at times like right now. We know each other enough for him to realize who I am. He does not expect me to react differently. It is just his way of wrestling with the idea of accepting God and all that comes with a commitment to God. Let's see where this goes. He looks a bit uneasy. His lips are twitchy. I think he is fighting against saying something. Oops, he's about to speak again.

Thomas continues: Jim, I tried this religion thing once. I went to a church and the people did not seem friendly or appear to care about anyone else. They seemed to get along with each other fine. But no one spoke to me. No one even followed up on my visitor's card. I never heard from them even though I checked the little box for contact.

Jim: **Thomas, did you speak to anyone there?**

Thomas: Ahem! Umm. Well, no.

Jim: **Thomas, you found the group that you fit in. You are just like them. You didn't extend fellowship to them, either. You really are one of them.**

Thomas: Aw, they're all just a bunch of hypocrites.

Jim: **My wife says, "I had rather go to church and be with a few hypocrites than go to hell and be with all of them." Besides you should go to church to worship God. It's not for your pleasure. It is for God.**

Thomas: I want control of my life here on earth.

Jim: **Thomas, are you sure you know how to have control? Several years ago my wife and I rented a house in Nashville, Tennessee. Springtime came and we realized that we would need a lawn mower to take care of the yard. We didn't have a mower and not much money, either. My wife spotted a special price on a lawn mower for which we had just enough money to buy it. I got in the old exhausted Volkswagen Beetle and chugged off to the store. By the way, this Beetle represented most of our potential wealth at the time. That is, it had future insurance claim money just ahead on the horizon. A little later, two different people on two different occasions crashed into the Beetle. The Beetle was already reshaped in a non-original appearance with an array of dents and rust spots visible from all sides. I just pocked the insurance money when it came in without repairing the Beetle. A little later I sold the Beetle for $100. Anyway, I get to the store expecting to purchase the mower. The clerk treated me poorly. So, like many of us, I got mad and left without the mower. After listening to my sad tale, my wife asked me "how I was going to cut the grass." She extended to me her hand scissors as she said, "Do you want to use these? Are you gonna let some jerk clerk keep you from getting something we need? Why don't you go back to the store and get what we need?"**

Thomas: What did you do?

Jim: **I went right back to the store to the same clerk. I handed him the money and told him I would pull my car around to the door so he could bring the mower out and** load it my car. You should have seen the look on his face when he saw the Beetle. If you ever saw one of those Beetles in the late 1950s you can envision the challenge associated with putting a lawn mower in the back of one of these small samples of an automobile. He asked if I was going to help him. I told him I would hold the door open for him and that he should be careful not to scratch the paint on my car. Again, the look on his face was a treasured look I will long remember. He must have really needed his job or he would have mowed the hair right off of my head, based on the look he gave me. You could see the virtual action in his eyes. Yes, he got the mower loaded in the car and hurried back into the store. I cheerfully chugged back home and mowed the lawn realizing that my wife had taught me a lesson on life management. You just can't let somebody else effect your life if you want control yourself. We all need to seek that which is best for ourselves rather than letting others direct our thinking and actions.

RetroClipArt.com

Thomas: Jim, you have made your point about letting others control who you are. I agree with you on that point. But you are just too legalistic on this obedience matter. You "hard sell" too much. You and many so called Christians are inflexible. Everybody is simply not the same.

Jim: **Careful Thomas, you may be missing something here. I used to think that way until I realized that these inflexible Christians you speak of really care for you and me. They are not trying to control us. They are trying to rescue us. You are imputing a false motive on their part. Besides, I don't think that God appreciates your reference to His Directives as "legalistic." He has not forced His Guidelines upon man at all, just the consequences of disobedience. Surely you do not practice derision by viewing those who follow God's Directives by referring to such obedience as being legalistic. This flies directly in the Face of God. I suggest that you back off this position quickly.**

Jim continues: **Too, you are accusing God of being inflexible. When you say that I have no empathy or love you are wrong. Love does not excuse. Love rescues. You think that you are throwing your words at people like me when it is God's position that you are attacking. You better give this one some further thought.**

Thomas: Jesus spoke against legalism when He was on earth.

Jim: **That makes our discussion more important. Jesus was speaking of those who placed requirements on people that God had not made. Jesus Christ condemned the**

practices of the religious leaders of His day, saying: "They worship me in vain: their teachings are but rules taught by men. You have let go of the commands of God and are holding on to the traditions of men." And he said further to them: "You have a fine way of setting aside the commands of God in order to observe your own traditions." {Mark 7:7-9} **The people you are speaking of do not represent what God has to say. They are false leaders masquerading as agents of God.**

Jim continues: **And Jesus was speaking of some misapplications of rules that God did make; some of which were discontinued by God's New Covenant with mankind. The first covenant was inferior to the new covenant.** {Hebrews 8:6-8} **Jesus was the mediator of the new covenant** {Hebrews 12:24} **by which we can be made free from the law of sin and death.** {Romans 8:2} **Notice that all these scriptures refer to laws and provisions for contractual performances. When we think of obedience as compliance with provisions of a promise between two parties then the word "legalism" loses its sting of derision. Those who encourage us to abide by God's offer of a covenant relationship are simply attempting to help us comply with God's provisions, not those of mankind.**

Thomas: Jim, stop it. I just want to be happy here and now.

Jim: **Thomas. This world is not my home. I'm just passing through. Like the astronauts, I am preparing to take a trip into the heavenly places, but I am headed toward a known destination where God has prepared a permanent room in**

His House for me. God created me for permanent, eternal existence to fulfill His Purposes, not mine or yours.

Thomas: For gosh sakes, Jim. Do you understand what you are saying? You are nuts!

Jim: Yes, Thomas. I am somewhat enthusiastic about what God has told me. Knowing the future helps me with the present. This, too, will pass so I must accept the present and prepare for the future. God has taken care of everything that really matters now and forevermore.

Thomas: God hasn't told you anything. You have never seen God. How could you claim to have interviewed God?

Jim: That may be the easiest question to answer that I have ever heard you ask. Just think, Thomas. Did you watch Columbus sail to America? Did an eye-witness tell you in person what Columbus did? You do believe that he did sail to America, don't you? Do you believe any history at all? Of course, you do. You read about it in books. You hear others testify about things you did not see in person. Through these means we learn of what has happened apart from our presence. The Bible is how God speaks to us today. He is the same God as He has always been. He has not changed. Neither has His Word as recorded in the Bible.

Thomas: But Jim, you said you interviewed God. Doesn't that mean that you asked Him questions as in a dialog?

Jim: **It's simple. When you consult a book, especially a dictionary, you search the book for the answer to your inquiry. God has already written out His Answers for us in His Bible, just like a dictionary. I may think out-loud sometimes as you heard me muttering just a bit earlier. I formulate my questions and then I read God's answers in the Bible. I repeat His Answers several times so that His Words become my understandings rather than those of my own creation.**

Jim continues: **Some people engage in conversations only to say what they wish to say without understanding what others are saying. They call it "taking turns." I never take God's Turn. I ask questions, but I never tell Him anything. I work hard at listening to His Word in the Bible. His Word is the Final Word, always and forevermore.**

Thomas: I don't doubt you Jim. You seem to have something I don't have. You seem content about it. Your unselfish approach to the Word of God has convicted me. I'm not like you yet, but I want to know more about God's way. Can I join you in the next session?

Jim: **Of course. God has already invited you and everyone else to join in. We will need to let God guide us with many of the questions we need to have answered. We will need to understand His Answers rather than seek our turn to talk. Let's not rush to conclusions until we have allowed God to reach us with His Word. Besides, it would not be polite to push "political correctness" of this world on Him.**

Jim continues: **I think we need to get clear on what listening and obeying God really means. Maybe, a good word to focus on for our understanding would be "compliance." It means acquiescence that is to give in to some "will" other than your own. To "acquiesce" means to "grow quiet," to consent without protest. (Just check any dictionary.) It does not mean "punishment" or "payment" for anything. Think how many times we comply with the ordinances of government on earth. We fill out many forms of compliance, we observe the laws of our communities, and we cooperate on so many things that are necessary to a safe and orderly life on earth. We are not earning our citizenship with these acts of compliance. But they are conditions for the exercise of our uninhibited citizenship. Citizenship in God's Kingdom requires the same needs for compliance according to the covenants of God. It is an agreement, a compact with God according to His Will for our best interest.**

Thomas: I'm ready.

Jim: **Bring your questions and be prepared to repeat after God. Just dump all your confusions and frustrations as soon as possible. There are better answers. And God has all of them for you and for me. We may need to let God help us with the questions. We may not be aware of something we need to understand. We may not know about it at all, or we may have it wrong. We will need to pray.**

Jim continues: **You should try that church visit again. If you were physically sick you would go to a hospital wouldn't** you? You would expect to find other sick people there, too. Maybe all the people who saw you at church were in the same condition as you. They may have been seeking instead of providing to others, just like you. Besides, God commanded us to assemble to worship him and to encourage others to do the same. {Hebrews 10:25} Worship is not about pleasing people. It is all about glorifying God. It is about seeking His help in faith. The early Christians met together on the first day of the week to worship God. It is important to separate corporate worship from individual worship. Privately we can go into our closet for prayer and we can individually worship God with instrumental music, as David did, provided that is one of our talents. But in the assembly on the first day of the week they did all things in common. During this assembly they did at least five common things in which they all took part:

1. Each observed communion. {Acts 20:7}
2. Each contributed as purposed. {First Corinthians 16:1-2}
3. Each sang songs cheerfully, making melody in their hearts, always giving thanks to God for everything. They did this together. They sang to each other and unto God. {Ephesians 5:19-20} They sang with their spirit and with their mind which carries the same conscious thought as prayer. {First Corinthians 14:15} They did not sing for entertainment. Important note: There is no reference to instrumental music in the assembled worship found in the Bible. It is only found in David's private worship.

4. **Prayed.** {Acts 8:5}
5. **Preached the Gospel (teaching and learning together.)** {Ephesians 5:19-20}

God's love is about rescuing and protecting all mankind. Fellowship among Christians is about encouragement, loving and caring for each other. Worship is clearly focused on praising God. One only needs to browse the Book of Revelation to discover that the whole heavenly host is seen praising God for His power over the evil forces of Satan as He has extend grace for those who those who faithfully behave according to His Will. There is clear victory and there is certain salvation as a result of God's love for His creations in heaven and earth.

Thomas: See you soon Jim.

Jim, thinking: ***That's encouraging. I will continue to write this book as Rich suggested. Thomas is showing me what I should do, too.***

Closing scene: Jim and Thomas leave, but God left the light on for everyone. The Bible is on the table and the stream of sunlight is still seen as flowing through a window shown about the Bible as a solid arch or vault.

16

SESSION 2: WHO AM I GOD?

(Simulated)

RetroClipArt.com

"I really need to know!"

Scene: The same two chairs and table are in the room in the same position. The Bible is on the table and the stream of sunlight is still seen as flowing through a window shown about the Bible as a solid arch or vault. The vault is surrounded by a similar dispersion as before of colors created by portions of the sunlight passing through trees just outside the window and the prism effect of the window panes. The Bible is not open this time, as if it is waiting to be opened.

Jim is sitting in one chair seemingly calmer than before. The other chair is empty, apparently awaiting Thomas this time. It is now realized that God will not need a chair.

Again, a soft breath of fresh air circulates in the room. As before, Jim looks around for a couple of minutes, enjoying the pleasantness of the moment.

Jim thinks as he looks at the Bible: ***I don't need to wait on God this time. I know He is already present.***

Then, suddenly as if to join Jim in this splendor, Thomas enters the room.

Thomas, first looking at Jim and then turning his eyes toward the Bible: Hello Jim! Hi God!

Jim, thinking: ***I hope Thomas is getting with the program now. He tends to be somewhat cavalier. God probably knows that and loves him anyway. Me too, I hope. Now let's hope that all of us make it through the hoop of truth in this session.***

Jim: **Nice to see you Thomas! Where would you like to start?**

Thomas: Like many people, I am okay in acknowledging God. I just don't seem to really understand man in relationship with God. Why should I exist with such a high probability of failure? Did I create myself? If God grieved that He had made man on the earth then why did He do it? {Genesis 6:60} What good am I? Why am I subject to such severe punishment? It seems unfair to me. If I have freedom of choice why doesn't God let me go my way forever without consequences? Why can't I just mind my own business and seek my own destiny? So far it seems like picking up a hot piece of iron with my bear hand. I just can't hold onto the hot iron. Consequences take the heat right out of my hand. I let go of the hot iron as a reaction rather than as a choice. That's a no brainer. There's no choice in that at all. It just seems to me that I am held hostage by God.

Jim talks and thinks: **Wow Thomas! You just took out the "sur" in "surreal" and made it all the way to the "core" of existence itself. We definitely need to let God handle these questions. Let's allow God to answer these questions in His way.** ***I hope that we are not being presumptuous. But I think these questions are fair as I believe that God would like for us to understand and mean what we do as He sees the mind of our souls.*** **Maybe the first question to God should be: "Why did you make carnal things if they are not pleasing to you now?"** ***I hope this is the best starting point. Hopefully, God views this as a good question even though He might not say so.*** **Let me pose the question to God: "God why did you make the earth and us along with it?" You didn't need earth. You had heaven. You really** didn't need us either. You had the angels to serve You. So why did You create anything outside of Heaven?

God answers: **King David asked essentially the same question: *"When I consider Your heavens, the work of Your fingers ... what is man that You are mindful of him, the son of man that You care for him?"*** {Psalm 8:3-4}

God continues: **You mentioned in your question, it wasn't because I needed anything. Yes, I made the world and everything in it**. {Genesis 1:1-25} **Yet I am not served by human hands, as if I needed anything**. {Acts: 17:24-25} **I was not lonely. Long before you were here, I already had "company" with My Son and the Holy Spirit along with a host of angels. We made you in Our Own Image**. {Genesis 1:26-27}

God continues: **The answer you need to understand is love, plain and simple. Despite not needing you, I chose to create you anyway, out of My great love: *"I have loved you with an everlasting love*.**" {Jeremiah 31:3}

Jim almost repeating God as he speaks and thinks: Yes, You loved us before You even created us. *I was already in His Plan from everlasting to everlasting. In the mind of God I have always been there wrapped in love. It's impossible to get my head around that idea, but its true; that's what "everlasting" love surely means.* You are love {First John 4:8},

and because of that love and Your wonderful creativity, You made us so we can enjoy all that You Are and all that You have done.

Jim, thinking: ***That reminds me of Papa Jim. He was always sharing the produce from his bountiful vegetable garden with his neighbors. He knew how to grow things so well. And Mama Artie could push a stick in the ground and we would see a beautiful flower spring forth for her to share with the ladies there about. They both seemed to enjoy seeing the pleasure of their neighbors as they enjoyed their gifts. God has said that "it is more blessed to give than to receive."*** {Acts 20:35} ***In this case, God is the most blessed of all because He gives the most of all. Papa Jim and Mama Artie showed me who God is and why He created us and placed us in a garden to enjoy His doings. Even though we disappointed Him through our disobedience, He has extended mercy and grace to those who have faith and obey Him.*** {Ephesians 2:8} ***He has promised us a place in Heaven where there will be no curse. There we will find the tree of life standing on each side of the river of life that flows from His Throne. The leaves of the tree are for the healing of nations. The tree will bear its fruit every month, twelve times a year.*** {Revelation 22:1-5} ***Those who over-cometh evil will be allowed to eat the fruit from this tree.*** {Revelation 2:7} ***He created us to enjoy His Home as He will share it with us. Apparently, He intends to enjoy our happiness in Heaven, rather than here on earth. It's not surreal folks. It's the real thing! That's His plan even before we were created.***

Thomas showing signs of doubt: But what are we good for?

God answers: **You are My workmanship. Dare anyone to question My doing**. {Job 38} **I only created that which was good**. {Genesis 1} **You were created in Christ Jesus to do good works, which I prepared in advance for you to do.** {Ephesians 2:10}

God continues: **First and foremost, you are to love Me with all your heart and with all your soul and with your entire mind.** {Matthew 22:37-38} **Second, you are to love your neighbor as yourself**. {Matthew 22:39}

Jim, thinking: *Love compels one to do for others. I see it in my family and friends. I feel propelled when I do things for others.*

God: **There's a war going on with Satan. Satan sinned, so I cast him and all his angels out of heaven onto earth**. {Revelations 12:9}

Jim, thinking: *Satan must have thought he could be a "big cheese" like God. The key here is that Satan was not a creator like God. Rather he is a destroyer.*

God continues: **Satan is walking about seeking whom he may devour.** {First Peter 5:8} **He thought he could claim Job, but he didn't get it done.** {Whole Book of Job} **I want you to be like Job. Jesus**

has done His part by resisting the temptations of Satan. {Matthew 4:1-11} **He destroyed death on the cross and brought life and immortality to light.** {Second Timothy 1:10} **Jesus destroyed Satan's work** {First John 3:8} **and his power over death.** {Hebrews 2:14-15} **Now, I need for you to stand firm against Satan so that you do not get enlisted in his army.** {Ephesians 6:10-18} **I need you to point people to Me through my Son Jesus Christ so that they may be reconciled to Me. When people put their faith in Me, they also defeat Satan and his lies.** {Ephesians 6:10-18}

Jim, thinking: *That's like voting for God instead of Satan. God wants our votes along with a commitment to His Campaign to destroy all evil. Our campaign commitment is exercised through righteous living as we stand against Satan wearing the whole armor of God. We are valuable to Him. We can play an exciting part in His loving, eternal plan. Suffice it to say that God, in His infinite wisdom, chose to make us a part of His eternal plan. How we live our lives on earth is an essential part of God's Plan. The Bible is full of instructions for how we should live our temporal lives. This is so, because we reside in the battlefield on earth that Satan seeks to conquer. If Satan and God, both, want us, we must have some value.*

Thomas: Jim, I heard your thoughts as you do tend to mumble out loud when you are thinking. You got it right. That's got to be correct and we shouldn't doubt it one moment.

Jim, speaking to Thomas: **It's all about choices. Looks like God chose us first. So it would seem good to be on the same side with God. He has already chosen us. However, God is going to have His Way with or without us. I think we better be counted as in with God.**

Thomas: Cool! Yep, I'm in too. The other side looks like a "hot iron" to me. That's a no brainer for me. When I think about it, there's no other acceptable choice at all. We should not depend on mortal men, "who cannot save." {Psalms 146:3} Looks like a desirable "free-gift" to me. I doubt that Satan has any real power anyway. It appears that He will be bound for a thousand years and then cast into the lake of fire and brimstone where he and his followers shall be tormented day and night for ever and ever. That doesn't sound like the winning team to me. {Revelation 20:7, 8, 10}

Jim, speaking to Thomas: **I just don't see any other answer that connects existence to us as clearly as these understandings. By the way, I am beginning to doubt that you are a doubter when it comes to the crux of the matter. You seem to be onboard.**

Thomas: Jim, I am still a bit worried about what may happen to me?

God, responding to Thomas: **There are only two possible places in eternity, when your life as a human has ended. One is in Heaven** {Second Corinthians 5:1; Second Timothy 4:18}**, a place of joy, peace, and happiness. It is where the saved live with Me**

forever {John: 14:1-3}**. Then there is also a place called Hell** {Matthew 5:29; 10:28}**, a place of pain and sorrow. Everyone who puts other things above Me and My Will must be punished there forever** {Matthew 25:41; Revelation 20:8}**. Need I say more?**

Thomas: Jim, I think we need to pay attention to God!

RetroClipArt.com

God: **Jim and Thomas, listen. You do not own yourself. We created you and you escaped through sin. You became a sinner on your own. Jesus bought you back for a price that He paid for your sins. In your sins you were owned by Satan. Through the shed blood of Christ you were purchased by Him.**

Jim, thinking: *Guess I have never owned myself. I didn't have the power to create myself or live independently on my own earth anyway. What was I ever thinking about when I thought that I was an independent free-spirit? It's*

just not so no matter how much I want to be independent and self-reliant. I really am relieved that I am owned with love. That love is so powerful I feel safe and secure with such a trusted and powerful owner. I am not held hostage. I am held safe.

Thomas: One more thing. Is baptism really necessary? Should I do the same thing as the Ethiopian eunuch did as recorded in Acts 8:36?

God: **Yes, Thomas you should be baptized for the forgiveness of your sins** {Acts 2:38} **to be saved** {Mark 16:16; First Peter 3:21} **and get into Christ.** {Galatians 3:26, 27} **I have commanded it so.** {Acts 10:48} **Your sins will be washed away** {Acts 22:16} **and you will be added to the church of Christ.** {First Corinthians 12:13} **Christ did it Himself even though He had not sinned. He did it to fulfill all righteousness and to please God.** {Matthew 3:13-17; Mark 1:9-11; Luke 3:21, 22} **You need to go down into the water** {Acts 8:38} **in the name of the Father, Son, and Holy Spirit.** {Matthew 28:19} **It is a burial so you should be immersed in the water.** {Colossians 2:12; Romans 6:3, 4} **Rejoicing comes after baptism.** {Acts 8:39}

Thomas: If Jesus did not sin why would He be baptized?

Jim, speaking to Thomas: **I can answer that one: Jesus was baptized because:**

(1) He was pleasing God by His actions.

(2) He was endorsing the rite of baptism by giving us an example to follow as the right thing to do in order to fulfill all righteousness. It was the right thing to do so He did it. So should we. It is our response to God representing our cleansing from sin through the shed-blood of Jesus in preparation to appear in the presence of God. Before Christ was crucified only the high priest could enter into the Most Holy Place once a year, on the Day of Atonement, as he made a sacrifice to gain forgiveness for the sins of the people. The Most Holy Place was a place reserved in the temple by God for Himself. A heavy curtain hung in front of the temple room symbolically separating God from sinful people. On the cross Jesus took on our sins so that we could now appear before God without our sins. When Jesus breathed His last breath the curtain was suddenly torn in two from top to bottom to signify that we could now enter into the presence of God spotless of sin. {Mark 15:38} That should be reason enough for each of us to do likewise as Jesus did Himself,

(3) He was confessing sin on behalf of the nation, as Nehemiah, Ezra, Moses, and Daniel had done.

(4) He was showing support for what John was doing (baptizing for repentance.)

(5) He was fulfilling His earthly mission of identifying with our humanity and sin as He was inaugurating his public ministry.

(6) **He was identifying with the penitent people of God, not with the critical Pharisees who were only watching.**

(7) **He was the perfect man, did not need baptism for sin, but He accepted baptism in obedient service to the Father, and God expressed his approval.**

Jim, continues speaking to Thomas: **It is interesting to note in Mark 1:10-11 that we find all three members of the Trinity together: God the Father (Voice), God the Son (Jesus), and God the Holy Spirit (descended like a dove on Jesus) at this baptism.**

Thomas: *Can't I just sign a commitment card?*

Jim: **You can sign the card, but it won't save you. We read In First Peter 3:21 that baptism saves us. Mark 16:16 instructs us that those who do not believe and are not baptized will not be saved, they will be condemned.**

Thomas: *But do I need to be immersed?*

Jim: **Yes, it is a kind of burial and resurrection.** {Romans 6:4; Colossians 2:12} **The word "baptism" comes from the Greek language where it means to cover, to dip, or to immerse. It does not mean sprinkle or pour. (Sorry about that one. Just research it for yourself.)**

Thomas: *Looks like the Word of God is clear about baptism.*

Jim: **In my opinion,[46] baptism is essential to allowing God to rescue us from sin through His Son, Jesus Christ. Sin, if not forgiven, stops us from entering heaven.** {Galatians 5:19-21} **According to Romans 3:23 everyone has sinned and we all fall short of the glory of God. Our iniquities have separated us from God.** {Isaiah 59:2} **God's forgiveness frees us from sin's guilt and punishment.** {Psalms 103:12; Isaiah 43:25; Micah 7:19; Psalms 103:3; Colossians 2:13; First John 1:9; Isaiah 43:25; Jeremiah 31:34; Hebrews 8:12}

Jim continues: **As God just clearly explained above, you should want to be baptized because:**

- **Baptism is a condition of salvation.** {Mark 16:15-16; First Peter 3:20-21}
- **Baptism leads to forgiveness of sins.** {Acts 2:38} **(Who hasn't heard that one?)**
- **Baptism puts one into Christ and His death.** {Romans 6:1-4; Colossians 2:12}
- **In baptism one puts on Christ.** {Galatians 3:37}
- **Baptism is into Christ's body (the church.)** {First Corinthians 12:13} **(The church is the body of Christ. Christians are the family of Christ.)**
- **Baptism brings the Holy Spirit into our heart as the guarantor of our forgiveness, providing ongoing protection against our weakness.** {Galatians 4:6; Romans 8:26}

[46] Caution! Our opinions are outranked by God's Will.

Thomas: Wow! I need to get out of here and find some water for my baptism. I don't want to be hindered any further by my own hesitation.

Jim: **Thomas, that's great! Be careful after baptism because you can still fall. Two did in First Timothy 1:18-20. Others have and will fall.** {First Timothy 4:1-3; Galatians 5:4-7; Hebrews 3:12; Second Timothy 4:4-10} **This is especially tragic because, at this point, there is no further sacrifice for sins left.** {Hebrews 10:26} **When those who have been enlightened and received the Heavenly gift fall away they are subjecting Jesus to public disgrace.** {Hebrews 6:4-6} **However, there is good news in the 24th verse of Jude revealing that God is able to keep us from falling. Maybe, that is the reason we receive the gift of the Holy Spirit as our guarantor when we are baptized. However this is conditional on us faithfully believing the truth, rather than turning to false teachings. God can keep us from falling and He guarantees that if we remain faithful, He will bring us into His Presence and give us everlasting joy. When Christ appears, and we are given our new bodies, we will be like Christ (without sin before God.)** {First John 3:2}

Thomas: I like guarantees.

Jim: **Thomas, ability is not an unconditional guarantee. God is able, according to Jude, to keep every believer from stumbling, that is, from experiencing major moral or doctrinal failure. A key interpretive question here is whether Jude was conveying an unconditional guarantee that God will keep all believers from stumbling, or**

whether he was referring to a conditional guarantee which requires a certain response by individual believers. The idea that this is an unconditional guarantee appears to be biblically and practically absurd. One need only think of men like David, Solomon, Peter, John Mark, and Demas who stumbled badly to reject such an idea. Yet many theologians nonetheless suggest that Jude 24 is an unconditional promise.

Jim continues: **How can anyone propose such an interpretation? It is because they mistakenly understand Jude 24 to be a promise of perseverance and eternal security. I believe that many commentators have missed the mark badly on this one. Jude 24 calls for, but does not guarantee, our perseverance. Perseverance is our responsibility. God does not stand in on that one for us. And, it is not dealing with eternal security at all. God is not able to do anything which is not logically or morally impossible. (Examples of things God can't do include making a square circle, creating a stone too big for Him to lift, or doing anything evil.) There are myriads of things which have happened which God could have stopped from happening. Take, for example, the fall of Adam and Eve. God could have created them without an ability to sin; yet He didn't. He could have kept the serpent from tempting them; but He didn't. Consider three examples where the same expression "*God is able*" is used and where the possible result either never occurred or where it only occurred when a condition was met:**

(1) John the Baptist said, "*God is able to raise up children to Abraham from these stones.*" {Matthew 3:9}
(2) The author of Hebrews wrote, "*He is able to aid those who are tempted*" {Hebrews 2:18}; yet this aid is conditioned upon the one being tempted looking to Him in prayer with faith. {Hebrews 3:12-15; 4:11-16}
(3) Similarly, Jesus conditioned the healing of two blind men upon their answer to this question, "*Do you believe that I am able to do this?*" {Matthew 9:28}

The fact that God is able to do something does not unconditionally guarantee that He will do it. It may be something He never intends to do or which He will only do for those who respond as He commands. As we shall now see, the latter is the case in Jude 24.

The word "*stumble*" is a word which only occurs here in the New Testament. It refers to losing one's footing, stumbling, or falling. Clearly it is used figuratively here. While some suggest that only doctrinal slippage is meant, Jude was warning his readers about false teachers who were promoting both false doctrine and licentious living. {Jude 15-18}

The context makes it clear that Jude is encouraging believers to look to the One who can keep them from being duped by false teachers. Notice verses 20-23. To suggest that in verse 24 Jude was unconditionally guaranteeing his readers that they wouldn't be duped is to destroy the whole point of the letter. It was Jude's fear that his readers would be duped by the false teachers that prompted him to write this letter. {Jude 3-4}

The word "faultless" can, also, be misleading: "To present you faultless with exceeding joy." This expression is, I believe, why many commentators suggest that God guarantees freedom from stumbling. They see the word "faultless" and they conclude that eternal salvation must be in view. That is, however, a mistake. What is in view is the future judgment of believers, the Judgment Seat of Christ. That is the time when every believer will be presented by Jesus before the Father. Not all believers will be presented as "*faultless.*" Nor will all believers have "*exceeding joy*" at this event. Only believers who lived faithful lives will have such an experience. Compare Matthew 16:27; Mark 8:38; First Corinthians 3:10-15; 9:27; Second Corinthians 5:10; and First John 2:28.

The word "*faultless*" ("*amomos*") means "*without spot or without blemish.*" It sometimes is used to refer to complete sin-less-ness, as when it refers to Jesus Christ. {Hebrews 9:11; First Peter 1:19} However, it can also refer to an experience which is not sinless but which is yet pleasing to God since it reflects faithfulness to Him. For example, Revelation 14:5 refers to the 144,000 who were spiritually pure. They remained faithful and scripture says, "*No lie was found in their mouths; they are blameless,*" for they are without fault [*amomos*] before the throne of God. {Colossians 1:22 and Second Peter 3:14} The same idea, though using a different Greek word ("*anenkletos*"), is found in the requirements for elders in the church. Elders are men

who must be blameless in their experience. {First Timothy 3:10; Titus 1:6-7}

Exceeding joy awaits believers who do not lose their footing. There will be a special measure of joy for such believers at the Judgment Seat of Christ and forever thereafter. God rewards faithfulness and that is exactly what He is saying in Jude 24.

At the Judgment Seat of Christ, no excuses will be valid. We won't be able to legitimately blame the devil, our parents, our spouses, our children, our genes, illness, fatigue, society, circumstances, or God Himself. Nothing can "make us" stumble from the path of righteousness as long as we are faithful. God is able to keep us from stumbling while we maintain an obedient relationship with Him. If any of us walks away from God, we do so because we have failed to look to Him who is able to keep us from stumbling. {Romans 16:25; Second Peter 3:14-18}

Victory is possible in the Christian life because God is ready, willing, and able to sustain us through the temptations and trials we face. The question is not whether He is able to keep us from stumbling. Rather, the question is, will we continue to look to Him in faith and obedience?

Early on God found one man (Noah) to be righteous. {Genesis 6:9} **Noah had faith and through obedience saved the descendants of his family (mankind today) of his day from destruction. God used a flood to destroy all**

living things except those protected in the ark that God directed Noah to construct. {Genesis 6-8} Later, Sodom and Gomorrah was not spared from destruction because there was no one found there who was righteous. {Genesis 18-19} God was not pleased with mankind's disobedience on either of these occasions. The key to God's actions in both of these occasions is based on the existence of someone who is righteous. {Genesis 6:9}

Christians throughout history often find themselves in the midst of social ruin and personal danger. You may be experiencing this now. Some of these conditions happen when government fails to function for the good of all inhabitants or society just falls apart. Some people feel like the conditions of Sodom and Gomorrah are coming down on them. Some even feel that God is not protecting them. So the question arises: What are we to do? Seems to me that the best thing a Christian can do is seek righteousness so that God will find someone who is righteous and save the whole community. In the book of James, God tells us that "the prayer of a righteous person is powerful."

The key to being righteous is to remove all impurities from ourselves and obey God. It works like the process that turns impure water into pure water. We just filter out all the impurities and only the pure water remains. And we obey God as Noah did. At least God may have mercy on us and get us out of town to safety as He did Lot. Of course, Lot did not exactly live a pure life but God had mercy on him during this occasion. It would be nice if God saved

our whole community or even our entire country because He found you and me to be righteous.

Thomas: Jim, you really took off on that one. But I agree. If we fail to stay connected to God we could still lose it all. It would be tragic, indeed, for us to fail so close to the finish. I'm glad you took the extra time to explore the danger of apostasy.

Jim continues with a grin: **Thomas, don't make God be like the exasperated mother whose son was always getting into mischief. She finally asked him "How do you expect to get into Heaven?" The boy thought for a moment and said, "Well I'll just keep running in and out and keep slamming the door until God says, 'For Heaven's sake, boy, come in or stay out!'" "Make up your mind!"**

Thomas: Jim, I will not turn back. It just makes no sense to ignore the Word of God.

Jim: **Thomas, don't forsake the assembly of Christians on the first day of the week, either. That's where the forgiven sinners meet to encourage each other and to worship God together.** {Hebrews 10:25, 26} **There two types of worship. There's the common assembly where we worship in unity and the private times where we worship God alone, maybe in our closet.** {Matthew 6:6} **Before the crucifixion of Christ, God's people met on the Sabbath for common worship. Then according to the book of Acts they began to be called by a new name ("Christians") and began meeting on the first day of the week for common** worship together. According to Acts 2:42-47, they devoted themselves to the Apostles' teaching (preaching), to the fellowship (sharing), to the breaking of bread ("Lord's Supper"), and to prayer. They prayed with their spirit and with their mind; they sang with their spirit and with their mind. {First Corinthians 14:15-16} They contributed as much as they were able {Second Corinthians 8:3} what they had cheerfully decided in their heart to give. {Second Corinthians 9:6-9} It was no longer calculated as a percentage of their wealth.

God: **I am Spirit. You must worship Me in spirit and in truth.** {John 4:24} **Worship is not about you. It is not for your pleasure. You must be worshipful showing reverence for Me. The Israelites stood for a quarter of a day while they read from My Book of Law, and spent another quarter of a day in confession and worshiping Me.** {Nehemiah 9:3} **They stood up and praised Me as the Lord their God. You should show Me the same reverence as your God since I am the Lord your God, too.**

Thomas, seeming to be full of joy: *God, thank you!*

God, seeming to have the final word: **My grace is sufficient for both of you.** {Second Corinthians 12:9}

Jim closes the Bible and says to Thomas: That was a good session. Maybe this is enough for this book. I'll try to close this one down for now and begin work on the next book.

Thomas: That would be nice! What do you have in mind for the future?

Jim: **I think that God would like to talk about His Son, Jesus. I think the title will be: "Let Me tell you about My Son" or "The Greatest Love Story of All Time." Most fathers like to talk about their children. I will try to help Him do that for us in another simulation. Later, I might follow with "Okay God, I Submit so Lay All of Your Directives on Me Now." And then, maybe, write about things that are worse than death and how we endure such trials and tribulations without further failure. I may just wrap up a bunch of stuff under the title of "Building Our Faith" or "Faith Under Construction." I might go with "Circle the Wagons, the Siege Is On!" or "Bible Economics."**

Thomas: Great! I think I know who I am now. I was actually lost within myself, but now I have been found. I will listen to God more carefully and do what He says. I will listen and learn, I will strengthen my faith by believing and doing, I will repent for forgiveness of my sins, I will confess Christ, and I will be baptized as soon as possible. Good bye for now Jim.

Jim: **Thomas, don't forget to continue to study the Bible. Honest study of the Bible is high worship to God. It honors Him as the Creator who made us, and who alone can guide us and protect us eternally. His power and wisdom is not only greater than ours, it is absolute. We need to be careful in listening to anyone other than God. For every credibility gap there is a gullibility fill. Don't be gullible.**

Jim continues: **Thomas, see you in the next book. Good bye.**

Thomas leaves.

Jim, thinking: ***I can hear JR right now saying, "thank God he's stopped writing this book. It's about time he quit."***

Jim concludes his thinking: ***Amen for now!***

17

CLOSING WORDS

RetroClipArt.com

JR said *"there were already too many forewords, so why are you still writing?" "You have plenty of middle words, too."* Well, JR you are still reading aren't you? My friend, Rich is encouraging me to keep going. Thomas wants to continue, so why don't you come along with us further. Anyway, we still need to get some logical closure on this whole discussion before I close this book down.

The moral of the story thus far seems to be: since the earth and all things on it belong to the Creator, then God surely has the final word on everything He owns.

Adam's licensed and temporary sovereignty, and thus mankind's, comes with both responsibility and accountability. Adam was instructed to tend the Garden (a responsibility.) Adam was, also, instructed by God to not to eat of the fruit of the Tree of the Knowledge of Good and Evil, or the wages of this sin (disobedience) would be death. That is, Adam was accountable to God and would suffer consequences for disobedience. We are all descendants of Adam and, thus, inherit Adam's nature.

The writer in Ecclesiastes simplifies the meaning of temporary freedom when he says: *"Young man, do what you want, but know that for all your actions God will bring you into judgement."* {Ecclesiastes 11:9} He also advised young people to *"Remember now thy Creator in the days of thy youth."* {Ecclesiastes 12:1}

There are so many questions for mankind to consider in regards to life and death. These are tough questions and the Bible has some tough things to say about these subjects. It is obvious that we are already engaged in life. It is death and judgement that waits before us. Central to this issue is the relationship of the Sovereignty of the Creator God and the responsibility of created man. Therefore, a little thematic study on death from the first created man, Adam, down to present day mankind should help.

Where Does Man Fit?

While we cannot speak with certainty for God, we are able to reason how man, even in his rebellion against God, brings honor and glory to God. Reason suggests:

(1) God did not create man out of a need for fellowship. God is, and always has been, complete and satisfied within Him. His triune nature provides a fellowship of perfect unity among

Father, Son and Holy Spirit, and in God's presence is the heavenly host, who praise His Name continually.

(2) God did not create man out of a need to manifest His creative nature. The Seraphim and Cherubim were created by Him; the earth, all living creatures on earth, the heavens and the stars. He made them all according to His satisfaction.

(3) God did not create man out of a need to manifest His almighty power and His majesty above all. Nor to manifest His attributes of love, eternality, faithfulness, omnipotence, omnipresence, omniscience, transcendence, sovereignty, righteousness, and all other attributes. God is all these things in His being. He already has all of these.

Therefore, God must have created man for His pleasure and His glory. Because He created man in His image it is reasonable to say that, as image bearers of God, man was created to ***magnify God*** throughout all eternity.

Man was created to live and love like God, and even in man's sin God is glorified. When Adam sinned, God could have killed him immediately for his disobedience. Instead God manifested and magnified His mercy and His redemptive love. His amazing grace was magnified when God provided a Savior who would come and rescue fallen mankind and restore man's image to the reflective nature God had intended.

In addition to God's mercy and grace given to mankind, we also see God magnified in His purpose and plan that is from before time began. God knew that man would sin. God knew that He would judge man and curse the earth. And, God knew that He would restore all things to His perfect plan and for His pleasure.

When we read in Genesis 6:6 that *"the Lord was grieved that He had made man on the earth, and His heart was filled with pain"* we may have misunderstood what was driving God's pain. God was expressing the sorrow He felt for what the people had done to themselves, as a parent might express sorrow over a child who has gone astray. God was sorry that the people chose sin instead of an agreeable relationship with Him.

God then said in Genesis 6:7 *"that I will wipe mankind, whom I have created, from the face of the earth–men and animals, and creatures that move along the ground and birds of the air–for I am grieved that I have made them."* So, maybe, God was thinking that earth was not a safe place for people because it was a place where Satan could take hostages using deception. Since the animals and creatures were made by God for man, maybe, God was inclined to take all of them out of the reach of Satan to a safer place. So, He eventually sent Jesus and the Holy Spirit to rescue mankind and get them safely to Heaven.

The repentance of God here does not presuppose any variableness in His nature or purposes. Here we see God simply expressing feelings in human terms (an anthropopathy.) These Words of God presents the truth that God, in consistency with His immutability, has taken a changed position in respect to a changed mankind. This is clear proof that, though God's Divine Purpose for mankind is immutable, His Divine Nature is not impassible. He did, in fact, re-birth mankind through the actions of His Son, Jesus, who eliminated the results of sin for those who qualify.

It is the wickedness that increased to such a degree that it became intolerable to God. This is said to observe His great hatred to sin, and abhorrence of it.

God did not change His Mind or alter His Purposes. He changed the course and dispensations of His Providence. God determined to do, and did something similar to mankind, when we repent of anything and set out to change it. It's similar to a potter, when he has formed a vessel that does not please him. He is not satisfied so he takes it and breaks it in pieces and remakes it into a form that he is pleased with. Perfection does not allow tolerance for leniency at all. God had to remove the uneasiness in His Mind that mankind might eat of the Tree of Life and live forever on earth out of the reach of His Care. {Genesis 3:22}

In the fall of man, God is magnified throughout all things that happen in ways that would not have been if man had not been given a choice to love, honor and obey or to disobey and sin. So, we have a powerful and mighty God Who is Creator, Redeemer, Sustainer and Restorer. And we were created in His image in order to magnify Him as we live among sinners where God does not go Himself. His Son, Jesus, spent some time among us as one of us, but not God Himself.

Our purpose in life is to please God by living in a way that honors and glorifies Him, by being His steward and His ambassador on earth and by living in the right relationship with Him. Man's mission is to glorify God, and for God to enjoy mankind forever.

So how do we bring pleasure and glory to God? The answer is, whenever we worship God, praise His works, obey His commands and love and serve Him and our neighbors, we honor and glorify His name and He is pleased. We manifest God's love and magnify the power of God by our lives as we live according to His Will.

Genesis records Adam was made in the image of the Sovereign Creator God. {Genesis 1:26-31} So it should not surprise us that God's personal attributes are stamped to a lesser degree on His creation Adam. For example: the Creator can speak, therefore so can Adam. Man's Maker can think, so man would have no problem thinking.

But differences in these same attributes also show the ultimate power of God as compared to the limited power of mankind. When the Creator spoke a Universe appeared. Man's speech achieves little by comparison.

The God of Creation is a Sovereign Ruler so the one made in His Image must also have some sovereignty. This showed when Adam was given dominion over planet earth. Compared to His Creator's Sovereign power, Adam's power to exercise dominion is small, a mere reflection of the Maker's power. Likewise, since Adam is a created being, he is also a dependent creature, not an independent one. The realm of Adam's control is temporary. Adam's limited power was authorized, gifted and granted by the higher authority of the Ruler of the entire universe. Therefore Adam is dependent on the truly Independent Sovereign Creator who made all things. So are we.

In Genesis 3 we discover Adam chose to sin by rejecting the authority of the One Who is ultimately Sovereign. True to His word, the Creator God expelled Adam and all of us along with Eve from His presence. Decay commenced eventually resulting in the death of all forms of life on earth. God banned mankind from accessing the tree of life so we could not eat and live forever as human beings. From that point we began to physically reap the wages of sin as we were doomed to die. The physical death penalty had been imposed by the Creator and it was irrevocable. Man became a fallen sinner and all human beings descended from the first man will die because of our sin, you and I included.

But did you notice that Adam and Eve didn't die on the spot? God told Adam that he would toil painfully for his food by the sweat of his brow the rest of his human life. Adam would return to the ground, since from it he was taken. {Genesis 17-19} God said that

Adam was nothing but dust. Some believe that God slew an animal to provide garments of skin for clothing to conceal their nakedness. The first pair of humans was left alive only because an innocent animal without blemish had its blood poured out to produce a covering for their sin. Adam and Eve would have died there and then had not God accepted and chosen a sacrificial substitute that died in their place. I have no scripture to support this position by some. However, I can say that this substitutionary principle reappears time and time again. This principle is consummated by Christ, the final Lamb of God who died for mankind's sin.

The point often missed is that God apparently did not intend for Adam and Eve, along with all mankind, to live in human form forever. There were two important trees in the Garden of Eden: the Tree of the Knowledge of Good and Evil and the Tree of Life. God warned about the Tree of the Knowledge of Good and Evil. But God did not mention the Tree of Life until after the forbidden fruit of the Tree of the Knowledge of Good and Evil was eaten by Eve and Adam. After this happened, God said that He did not want them to eat from the Tree of Life which, apparently, would have allowed them to live forever in human form. {Genesis 3:22-24}

At this point decay set in which eventually results in death to the human body. Without access to God's source of sustaining life mankind is destined to die. {Hebrews 9:27; Ecclesiastes 8:8} God closed down the Garden of Eden completely so that Adam and Eve (thus, all mankind) could not access the Tree of Life. {Genesis 3:24} The Tree of Life now resides in Heaven (the paradise of God) where it will provide life to those who are saved forever. {Revelation 2:7}

This point becomes even more interesting when we realize that the Tree of Life was never mentioned in the Bible until it became a risk for God. So far, we have no authentic information that God gave instructions about this tree before the fall of Adam and Eve.

Yes, I said *"a risk for God."* Since God did allow Adam some sovereignty while residing among these trees in the Garden of Eden, Adam could choose to eat the fruit from any of them, including the Tree of Life. Through the granting of this sovereignty God took the risk of losing mankind to His enemies through rebellion. Satan was created by God; he exalted himself, rebelled against God, and became the enemy of God. {Second Peter 2:4; Jude 6; Matthew 25:41; First Timothy 3:6}

Now God says *"For our struggle is not against flesh and blood, but against the rulers, against the authorities, against the powers of this dark world and against spiritual forces of evil in the heavenly realms."* {Ephesians 12} Satan is the deceiver of the whole world. {Revelation 12:9} "Satan" means "enemy." {Job 1:6-12; Zechariah 3:1; Matthew 13:39; First Peter 5:8}

Adam and Eve probably could have eaten from the Tree of Life originally {Genesis 2:16}, but God gives no decree that they had to eat of it to sustain their life at that point. However, the tree may have been one means by which God used to help support and maintain life within Adam and Eve, perhaps a type of sustenance. God ultimately sustains all things {Colossians 1:17}, and if we look at the Israelites wandering in the desert for 40 years while their feet never swelled and their clothes never wore out {Deuteronomy 29:5}, we see a clear glimpse of what God can do. The fruit or leaves of the Tree of Life were not required for the Israelites in this case.

Also, keep in mind that the Bible gives no hint that they had to eat of this tree until after sin took place. After they sinned in Genesis 3, God sentenced them to die as per Genesis 2:17 and Genesis 3:19.

This was, in part, why they were forbidden to take from the Tree of Life at this moment. But consider God's statement here:

> Then the LORD God said, *"Behold, the man has become like one of Us, knowing good and evil; and now, he might stretch out his hand, and take also from the tree of life, and eat, and live forever"* {Genesis 3:22}.

This seems to imply that Adam and Eve could have eaten from the Tree of Life after they sinned and this would have provided them sustenance to live forever. Had they been permitted to eat from the Tree of Life, then they would have been forced to live eternally in a sin-cursed world. But God had a better plan in place: one of redemption in Jesus Christ with a new heaven and a new earth that would not be cursed. {Revelation 21:1-8; 22:1-5}

Actually, God is the source of all life. Even the Tree of Life is fed by God as the tree, itself, feeds from a pure river of water of life, clear as crystal, that proceeds from the throne of God and of the Lamb down the middle of the great city. The Tree of Life stands on each side of the river. {Revelation 22:1-2}

God is the only Savior {Psalm 62:6; John 14:6}, and through Him is the only way to live forever without pain and suffering. Thus, God stopped them from trying to attain eternal life in a sin-cursed world. God demonstrated His grace in refusing to allow mankind to live eternally in a world filled with sorrow and suffering. Instead, He has provided the way for us to enjoy eternal life in a place where there is no more death, sorrow, pain, or curse. {Revelation 21:3-4; 22:3}

When you look at the longer term picture you see Jesus preparing a place for each of us in Heaven. {John 14:2} Perhaps, Heaven has always been God's intention for our final destiny with a temporary layover on earth.

This contrast between the two trees suggests that mankind is more interested in testing warnings than heeding them. Some people cannot resist the temptation to test a sign that says, either, *"Dry paint"* or *"Wet paint"* or *"Do not touch."* Since there were no apparent instructions pertaining to the Tree of Life Adam and Eve were not challenged by the sovereignty behind a forbidden directive in regards to the Tree of Life. This emphasizes the nature of mankind to resist submission to authority when there are specific rules.

18

CONCLUSIONS

RetroClipArt.com

"Finally!"

The simple answer to the question, *"Why did God create a world He knew would turn against Him?"* God had a plan and a purpose from the very beginning. He planned to magnify His mercy and pour out

His amazing grace upon fallen man and a cursed creation through His Son, Jesus Christ. That plan and purpose will forever magnify His Name, throughout all eternity. One day at the mention of the name of Jesus every knee should bow and every tongue confess that Jesus Christ, the Son of God, is Lord to the glory of the Father, God. Because after Jesus fulfilled the Will of God in the salvation of mankind God exalted Jesus to the Highest Place. {Philippians 4:6-11}

Some Important Principles:

Principle number 1: God is solely eternally sovereign. There is no other God before Him or His equal. {Revelation 1:8; First Timothy 1:17}

Principle number 2: God created the earth and everything thereon or related, including mankind. {Genesis 1-2}

Principle number 3: God made man in His Own image so that he may glorify God through magnification. Man is an image bearer of God. {Genesis 1:26-28}

Principle number 4: The Sovereign God has made man responsible and granted him temporary, limited sovereignty on earth. {Genesis 1:26-28}

Principle number 5: Since the fall of man into sin, there has been a struggle between the sinless Sovereignty of God versus sinful man's rejection of submission, responsibility and accountability. We would much rather that mankind remains totally sovereign and let God take full responsibility for sin. Then we could dispense with submission and accountability. It shows in the various ways we tend to blame God for our sin. For example, some people with impure life styles claim God made them that way, regardless of the fact that the sovereign God said He didn't! {Genesis 1:31 and First Timothy 4:4}

Alternatively, we make Satan our excuse and claim *"the Devil made me do it."* A comedian named Flip Wilson masquerading as "Geraldine" portrayed this tendency of mankind to seek a slip-away from our misdeeds. Adam and Eve did the same thing. Adam blamed Eve and Eve blamed the serpent. {Genesis 3:12-13} Today some people blame an unfair socioeconomic environment for their thieving of unearned fruits, rather than working by the sweat of their brow. No matter what, it can't be our fault! People want more sovereign power to act, but less accountability for our actions.

Principle number 6: There are no minor sins. Jesus made this clear. He reminded us some 4,000 years later after the fall of mankind that if you break the least of His commandments you may as well have broken all of them. {Matthew 5:19} Therefore all sins matter. However, it is good to know that all sins except blasphemy against the Holy Spirit are forgivable. {Matthew 12: 31-32} This scripture addresses the case where the Pharisees had blasphemed against the Holy Spirit by attributing the power by which Christ did miracles to Satan, in the 24th verse of Matthew 12, instead of the Holy Spirit. It indicates a deliberate and irreversible hardness of heart. This is the only sin that is worse than all the others. Only those who have turned their backs on God and rejected all faith have any need to worry. Whoever rejects the prompting of the Holy Spirit removes him or herself from the only force that can lead one to repentance and restoration to God.

Principle number 7: We have been redeemed from the wages of sin and given a rebirth through the blood of the Son of God, Jesus Christ. This process is carried out in baptism as we are buried with Christ and raised with Him to newness of life through our faith in the power of God, Who raised Christ from the dead. {Colossians 2:12} Because Christ died for us, we have been crucified with Him. {Romans 6:2-13; 7:4-6; Second Corinthians 5:14; Galatians 2:20; 5:24; 6:14; Colossians 2:20; 3:3-5; First Peter 2:24} Our old, rebellious nature died with Christ (crucified). {Romans 6:6; 7:4-6; Colossians 3:9, 10} Christ's resurrection guarantees our new life now and eternal life with Him later (resurrected). {Romans 6:4, 11; Colossians 2:12, 13; 3:1, 3}

Since Jesus became a human just like us one might ask "how come He did not fail the same as the rest of us humans?" Answer: He was able to resist sin because He never forgot who He was and why He became human.

Regardless of our opinion, God has the FINAL WORD! And God is love.

RetroClipArt.com

"God Loves You Too!"

May the road rise to meet you.
May the wind blow at your back.
May the sun shine warmly on your face.
May the rain fall softly on your fields.
And until we meet again,
May God hold you in the palm of His hand.

—Irish Blessing

ABOUT THE AUTHOR

James Benjamin Edwards

"Jim"

Most importantly, the author is a member of the church that Jesus said in Matthew 16:18 that he would build. The Lord first added a large number to the church of Christ in the second chapter of the Book of Acts. Jim followed that group much later in becoming known as a Christian in the same manner as those in Antioch who were the first to be called Christians. He has served as a deacon and as an elder in local congregations; and as a volunteer minister to university students and soldiers in basic training.

Currently, Jim is focused on writing simulations portraying conversational-style dialog among those providing insights to issues most important to his life. While his top priority is God, he has other interests.

Of lesser importance, Jim is a Distinguished Professor Emeritus of Accounting in the Moore School of Business at the University of South Carolina. He holds B.B.A., M.B.A. and Ph.D. degrees earned at the University of Georgia. His professional certificates include: Certified Management Accountant (CMA), Chartered Global Management Accountant (CGMA), Certified Cost Analyst (CCA), Certified Computer Professional (CCP), Certified Internal Auditor (CIA), and Certified Public Accountant (CPA).

Jim has published more than 100 articles in professional publications; receiving eight national awards for his writings. He is the author or co-author of three books and served as assistant editor of *Managerial Planning* magazine for five years. In 1986 he conducted a special study for the National Commission on Fraudulent Financial Reporting, *"Expansion of Non-Audit Services and Auditor Independence."* He is a contributing author to *Evaluating the Performance of International Operations*, published in 1989 by Business International. He is the past editor of *Emerging Practices in Cost Management,* the *Handbook of Cost Management,* and the *Handbook of Cost Management for Service Industries;* all are annual publications by Warren, Gorham & Lamont, Inc. He is the editor of the *Journal of Corporate Accounting and Finance.*

Jim serves as a part-time business advisor specializing in small group and individual "strategic chats" or "strategic thinking retreats" and teleconferencing. He is an international business researcher, author, business architect, business advisor, and management development mentor. He, also, serves the legal profession in a "shadow" support role to attorneys as an evaluator of reports prepared by expert witnesses in financial litigation cases.

Past societal listings (1980s–1990s) include:

Marquis WHO'S WHO IN THE SOUTH AND SOUTHWEST
Marquis WHO'S WHO IN FINANCE AND INDUSTRY
Marquis WHO'S WHO IN AMERICA (re-nominated in 2016)
Marquis WHO'S WHO IN THE WORLD

Work experience includes corporate controller, partner in a CPA firm, vice-president of a data processing company, university professor, and consulting engagements.

Jim served eight years in the U.S. Marine Corps Reserve Program.